Fanny Says

❦

Poems by

NICKOLE BROWN

AMERICAN POETS CONTINUUM SERIES, No. 147

BOA EDITIONS, LTD. ❧ ROCHESTER, NY ☙ 2015

First Edition
15 16 17 18   7 6 5 4 3 2 1

For information about permission to reuse any material from this book please contact The Permissions Company at www.permissionscompany.com or e-mail permdude@eclipse.net.

Publications by BOA Editions, Ltd.—a not-for-profit corporation under section 501 (c) (3) of the United States Internal Revenue Code—are made possible with funds from a variety of sources, including public funds from the New York State Council on the Arts, a state agency; the Literature Program of the National Endowment for the Arts; the County of Monroe, NY; the Lannan Foundation for support of the Lannan Translations Selection Series; the Mary S. Mulligan Charitable Trust; the Rochester Area Community Foundation; the Arts & Cultural Council for Greater Rochester; the Steeple-Jack Fund; the Ames-Amzalak Memorial Trust in memory of Henry Ames, Semon Amzalak and Dan Amzalak; and contributions from many individuals nationwide. See Colophon on page 148 for special individual acknowledgments.

ART WORKS.
arts.gov

State of the Arts

NYSCA

Cover Design: Sandy Knight
Interior Design and Composition: Richard Foerster
Manufacturing: Versa Press, Inc.
BOA Logo: Mirko

Library of Congress Cataloging-in-Publication Data

Brown, Nickole.
[Poems. Selections]
Fanny says : poems / by Nickole Brown. — First edition.
    pages cm. — (American poets continuum series ; No. 147)
ISBN 978-1-938160-57-8 (pbk. : alk. paper) — ISBN 978-1-938160-58-5 (ebook)
I. Title.
PS3602.R72243A6 2015
811'.6—dc23

                                2014039935

BOA Editions, Ltd.
250 North Goodman Street, Suite 306
Rochester, NY 14607
www.boaeditions.org
A. Poulin, Jr., Founder (1938–1996)

Fanny Says

Note

This book is a biography of sorts, piecing together fragments left behind from Frances Lee Cox, my maternal grandmother from Bowling Green, Kentucky. Some names and details have been altered to protect the identity of those involved. All poems whose titles begin with "Fanny Says" and most lines in italics, unless otherwise noted, are not words I *wrote* but words I *wrote down*, transcribing best I could as my grandmother spoke to me.

Contents

III

IV

For Frances Lee Cox,
because she said so

For Our Grandmothers

All of them, who clutched their pocketbooks, who hid the money
for the light bill in the Bible, who counted, counted, and recounted

stacks of towels. For our grandmothers who stored the white wax
of bacon grease in a coffee can, who tossed table salt over their shoulders,

who had rules about stepping under ladders, eating supper's last
biscuit, and the acceptable distance hemmed up from a girl's knee.

For our grandmothers who would not let us call her *grandmother*, who wanted
to be called anything but *grandma*, for they were too young to be a mother

when they became mothers, and then?   You.

For our grandmothers who made us pick our own switch, who cooled
hot coffee on a saucer, then sipped from its chipped edge.

For our grandmothers who would not call a cicada a *cicada* but a *locust*,
a thirteen-year plague of them, making an apocalypse of June, for grandmothers who

considered a tabby not a *cat* but *a tail-switch hex* that would slip under your bedroom door,
take your breath from you, then smother the baby in its sleep.

For our grandmothers who taught there's a right way and a wrong way—
right is right, wrong's wrong—*ain't no sense in between*. For grandmothers

who emptied their husband's fish-gut buckets and bore enough children to run
out of names. For my grandmother, who snatched me from the nurse and wrapped me

in her tea-length mink coat. It was cold, almost spring, and though I was bruise yellow
with jaundice, she took us out of that hospital, settling her youngest daughter,

a teenage mother, careful in the back. With no shoulder belts or infant seats or air bags, it was simple: she held me up front for my first ride, she turned the key.

We were on our way, she took us
on home.

I

You shall know the truth, and the truth shall make you odd.
—Flannery O'Connor

Fuck

is what she said, but what mattered was the tone—
not a drive-by spondee and never the fricative
connotation as verb, but from her mouth
voweled, often preceded by *well*, with the "u" low
as if dipping up homemade ice cream, waiting to be served
last so she'd scoop the fruit from the bottom, where
all the good stuff had settled down.

Imagine: not a word cold-cocked or screwed to the wall
but something almost resigned—a sigh, an *oh, well,*
the f-word made so fat and slow it was basset hound,
chunky with an extra syllable, just enough weight
to make a jab to the ribs more of a shoulder shrug.
Think of what's done to "shit" in the South; this is
sheeee-aaatt but flicked with a whip, made a little more
tart. *Well, fuck, Betty Sue, I never did see that coming.*
Can you believe?

Or my favorite, not as expletive but noun—*fucker,*
she said, but what she meant was *darlin, sugar pie, sweet beets,*
a curse word made into a term of endearment, as in
Come here, you little fucker, and give your grandma a kiss.
If the child was young enough for diapers, he'd still be a *shitass,*
but big enough to lift his arms and touch his hands together
over his toddling tow head, he was *so big,* all grown, *a cute little*
fucker, watch him go.

Fuck is what she said, but what she needed
was a drum, a percussion to beat story into song, a chisel
to tap honey from the meanest rock,
not just *fuck if I know* or *fuck me running* or *fuck me*
sideways or *beats the fuck out of me* but said tender,

knowing there was only one thing in this whole world
you needed to hear most: *You fucker you, don't you know*
there wasn't a day when you weren't loved?

If you still don't understand, try this: a woman
up from poor soil, bad dirt, pure clay. A woman as
succulent, something used to precious little
water, hard sun. Rock crop maybe, threading roots
to suck nutrients from the nothing
of gravel, the nothing of stone, a thriving thing
sturdy, thorned, green out of mere
spite and, because you least expect it,
laughing, cussing up a storm—my grandmother
who didn't ask for power but took it
in bright, full, fuck-it-all bloom.

Your Monthly

is what her mama called it. But what I want is a word for the year she bled
freely, a wad of old washrags, each end pinned to a belt around her waist,

a word for twelve happy deaths, each unfertilized cell that washed out
saying, *Not yet, Fanny, you still just a child yourself,* because this world knows

a girl of fourteen's too old to be playing Cowboys and Indians but also knows
how young she was when, stiff red feather in her hair, she scrambled inside hollering,

Mama, come quick, I'm bout to bleed to death. A word for the year she learned to walk
in red shoes pulled from some rich lady's trash, the sound of those heels down the hall

two guns cocking with quick clicks, a sound to hide from her daddy in the morning
eating his breakfast of milk and cornpone with a spoon. A word for the time before

a man swaggered in, bought her a dime-store Coke, bought her very first bra, then took her
to the picture show to see a cartoon with dwarves impossibly happy to be working the mines.

A year later, she was expecting—*though what exactly I was expecting,* she told me,
I couldn't have said. A word, please, somebody give me, for that season with her uterus

small and tight as an inedible green pear, her body keening and cramped in its stall.
A word for all things not yet stretched to bits, a word for all things not yet broken,

a word for all things left unbroken, a word for breakable yet unbroken things,
a word for unbroken, expectant things. Tell me, what is that word?

Fanny Says She and Her Husband Had Their First Fight

Well, I was throwing fried potato sandwiches and he was throwing fried potato sandwiches, and little Barry, my firstborn, he was a year old and having a good time, throwing some potato too. But mind your grandfather only threw but one, and it smacked me square in the face, but only oncet.

See, I was angry because for months and months Monroe had been promising me ten dollars for a dress, and so I asked him, *Can I have my ten dollars now?* And he said, *No.* And I asked him why, and he said he was going to buy a saw. Well, that's when I called him a lying son of a bitch and threw my sandwich.

But he said, *That dress, that dress ain't gonna get us nowhere. But these hands, these hands and that saw's gonna get you a dress and then another dress and then a dress after that.* And he always did promise he'd do good by me, and he did, eventually. But I wanted my dress. But he bought the saw, and that's the way it was, always choosing the saw over me.

Fanny Linguistics: Malapropisms

A language is a dialect with an army and navy.
                                    —Max Weinreich

Unpack *chester drawers* to find
chest of drawers,
        Tandalon to   *Tylenol,*
            furrl   to   *foil,*
                gazebo pills to   *placebo,*
                     salmonella candles to   *citronella,*
and when the cousin who shoots frogs out of trees with a pellet gun
graduates first in class,
        congratulate him not for being *Valedictorian*
                but for being *Crowned Victoria.*

Never drop the friendly *s* in *anyways,*
and when Monroe belts out
"In the Pines" at full vibrato
from the roof, he'll stop his hammering
long enough to yell down
for *rim-rams* and *tim-tams.* Best always do what your grandfather says,
        don't come back
from the hardware store without them
even if not one soul—not clerk or handyman or contractor—
        knows what the hell he's sent you to buy.

Not a family for quiet things, the silent
consonants were
varmint traps, bad mayo barfed up
        with the *toe-main* poisoning,
running hot and cold with a full-on case of
        the walking new monayah you'll bout never recover from.

It's like that snotty *b*   in *subtlety*—
that sorority chick—her tennis skirt, the white snake
of her ponytail hissing back and forth
to remind you:

       you'll always lose the game, and despite all it,
       your daddy's money never was good enough—
       he never could get us in the club.

So rarely one for airs, we swung
the racket like a bat, aimed the ball
for the familiar hills to answer her plain:

    Then fuck suttle.

Fanny Says She Spent It

Betty Sue, now—yes, my sister Betty and me—we were tight. She came over my house nearly every day, and I was the one taught her how to steal checks, you see. So we'd wait till the men went off to the track, and we'd go shopping—$1,000 a piece—but we didn't care. I mean, what made the men think we should sit around all day while they were out, just a gambling away? Shit. They'd catch us on Monday, but it was too late. Wurn't a thing they could do about it.

Yes, he made it, and I spent it. He fixed one house, then another, then another, and then he built one house, then another, then built another. All them churches and condos and more houses to boot. Yes, all those homes with people living in them and no one even knows now that Monroe poured their foundation. But half of Louisville's got his name on it. He made all that money, more than we ever could have wanted, and we spent it, every last dime.

Ain't no sense in holding on to it; you know and I know you can't take it with you when you go.

Pepsi

1.

Because she thought even fish said something about class.

Catfish, for example—mud-blooded, fried up only by men who
mow lawns and scrape shingles and make their living shoveling
dirt under their nails—

but bass? Bass were wild, wide-mouthed, pink throats hooked
by men with enough money for a boat, flashy catch with heads to be taken
by the working man who works the other men.

And trout? We heard about men who ate a fish called *rainbow*,
but they were freezing their nuts off up north, hip-deep in icy water,
reciting poetry, casting houseflies across a stream.

So why should soda be any different?

RC, that's for overall-wearing kids with runny eyes,
a once-a-month Moon-Pie treat after borrowing the family's
one pair of shoes and huffing five miles to the general store.

And Coke? Chugged by the common freckle-face gal across the river
in Indiana—a Hoosier who hived her hair and squeezed
all she could please into polyester skirts—
Lord, look at her in her Sunday best; she actually thinks she looks good.

Pepsi though? Well, Pepsi was enough for Joan Crawford,
Pepsi was a bitch who knew how to ash with two taps from a two-inch filter,
not one nicotine stain on her manicured hands.

Pepsi knew how to stroll in Italian heels, how to pin a hairpiece
at her crown and let it waterfall into an aerosol nest
of natural, how to glue a strip of lashes to her *you-got-that-right* wink,
knowing just how easy it is to get a man
and just how hard he is to keep.

2.

Because the sound of the first can
in the morning was the sound
      of nectar
           firecrackered,

sugar sent up
      to the sky, dull liquid
           kissed with foam, the sound of ready oil
                excited by flour, your gravy being made.

Because in a sweating glass,
      it cooled
           her knot of hot sleep
              to the same crisp

as the air-conditioned room.

Because it was the secret
      of lemon and orange and vanillin
           tickling the air, a fizz that
              whispered,

Wake up now, Fanny,
      your bad flashing night is through.

3.

Because she was loyal—downright militant—to things she loved, Pepsi was all

she would drink. Rarely water, not juice, not milk, and damn straight, no trailer-trash
beer. She might have coffee later, before her shows came on, but this was the drink
that woke her, the drink that kept her up.

Should you fix her a glass, you might get the full Pepsi Lecture, her obsessive
counting game, because there was a hell of a lot she couldn't control, but she could
control this:

Make it four pieces of ice—not three, and not five. But four. And I don't want it too full;
don't make me spill it all over myself. And use a six-ounce glass, not some big suck-o jug,
not a little old juice glass, but six ounces, that big. I want that glass to be plastic and pretty,

something with flowers, maybe in pink; now, don't give me no ugly cup.
It better be clean too; don't give me no dirty glass, pull it hot from the washer if you have to,
but just four—count them, four—cubes of ice.

4.

Because years later
in the hospital
we lost her
in the deep folds
of a coma
for days,
and when she finally
woke, she was
confused, looked
around, asked,
What are you all here

staring at me for?

[24]

Her oldest answered,
Because,
Mama,
we need you.

Well,
okay then,
she said.
Quit
being so useless,
standing around.

Somebody pour me
a fresh Pepsi?

5.

Because it was not water pulled from the well, water from a place with no pipes,
because it was not so rich in iron that washing was like taking a bucket shower in blood.

Because it was not a chipped Mason jar lukewarm from the neighbor's tap.

Because it was not milk with a layer of unhomogenized creaming the top,
because it was not tea her mama set out on the porch to brown in the sun.

Because it was not Bowling Green, not western Kentucky, and there's no need
to ever wait again for the mule pulling the ice man.

No, you have a pocket full of change now, Fanny. It's 1944 again, no sense
scuffling your feet, standing outside on the hussy corner of the dime store.

You walk right in, order straight from the fountain if you want.
You're in Louisville now, you have yourself a man, you'll never have to choke down

anything flat again.

Fanny Says Sometimes It's Worth the Whupping

I remember the first time I seen the sign: *Air Conditioned.* It was at the movie theater, the one for all the rich people. And I said to myself: *What's that?* Well, I didn't know what it was, but I said to myself, *Well, we'll just find out then.* And so I stole the eleven cents from my sister Evelyn's purse to get in, and after school, I walked in and just couldn't believe it . . . it was a double feature, and all that cool, crisp air. It felt so good on my body I thought I was gonna die. And I sat in the middle, right like now in front of the tee-vee—a straight line—not too far to one side or to the back or the front where I had to bend my head all back or I'd walk out—I was a bitch now, always was—but sat right in the middle. And boy, did it feel good.

Now of course when I got home, Mama asked, *Fanny* (they called me *Fanny*, never *Frances*, even then). She said, *Fanny, did you steal that eleven cents from Evelyn?* And I said, *Yes, Mama.* And she said, *Well, if you don't give it back, you know you're going to get a whupping now?* And I said, *Yes, Mama, I'll pay it back.* And so the next morning, I went across the street to Miss Peterson's (she was kind of snotty and never did pay no attention to us), and I stole three milk bottles off her front porch. You see, I knew I could take them up to the store and sell them for three cents a piece, and so I did.

That evening at suppertime, I had nine cents, but it didn't matter, because I got a whupping anyways. But it wasn't no big deal now, really, cause Daddy didn't really want to do it . . . he told me that, later, said that he had to do it—*for Mama*—and he'd fold a belt over, like this, and swat at my legs, never above the knees or at my butt or nothing, he wasn't like that, and I'd run around him in circles, screaming, *Daddy! Daddy! Daddy!* And he'd swat, but just barely, and it didn't hurt.

You know, one time, when I was about six, I forgot to cry and Mama said to him, *Topa, look at her face, she didn't even cry,* and he said, *Fanny, come here so I can whip you again* but he didn't really, but I worked up the best tears I could so that I wouldn't get no more.

Go Put on Your Face

is what she said, and what she meant was
a little somethin-somethin, a little dunka-dunk,
a little mascara and blush, gloss and perfume,
and *best conceal that stork bite*, that hot *V* that flared
between my brows, that red check pointing down
to my pink gum-flavored gum, chewed and blown and popped
with a flirt, me pulling it to string and twirling it with the tip,
just like a dumb blonde should.

Spit that gum out now, and hurry, go put on your face, we got to go,
she said because who knows who might see me at
the grocery eyeing glossies at the checkout, studying women
on the cover who don't let their self go, no, not for a second,
they keep their pretty selves up, they know how to contour,
how to highlight, how to erase their face into a foundation
to build new, how to shadow deep-crease shadows
in their *come-sit-your-handsome-ass-down-here* gaze.

I was taught: without your face put on
your face is a turnip jerked round and pale from mud,
that your face without your face put on is flat-footed,
a gal fanning herself with her own apron, a daughter
with eyes too far apart that don't know no better,
bless her heart. And what girl don't need a little color?
What girl don't need those tiny boxes of pressed powder to catch
sparks, those applicators and brushes and wands to change
her, saying you came from something even though you ain't from
nothing, saying a good man, he's gonna find you,
gonna keep you, and *someday, yes, someday, even a kitchen
all your own.*

You see, child? You listen to your grandmama.
Someday a kitchen all your own, the air so high
the cool will crank through the vents like money,
your husband coming home any minute now cause he works hard
for you and he's coming home to sheets
hot from the dryer and all that cool inside. He's
honey-I'm-home through the door and you're there, feet up,
cared for as a hothouse orchid,

pedicured and manicured and foil-bleached bright,
and if you want to keep him, best put on that face
every damn night.

For My Grandmother's Teeth, Pulled When She Was Thirty-six

You wanted teeth the color of milk
      warmed in a pan and wrist-kissed,
            teeth like tended white roses
                  cured of black-spot leaves,
but instead got bad gums,
      a loosened, receding
            smile not all the fluoride
                  in Louisville could save.

So by the time I was born
      all your teeth were nibs of bone,
            dead seeds scattered to the nostalgic
                  strata of iodine and Wonder
Bread bags, of glass
      baby bottles, metal
            highchairs, wooden
                  dairy crates—artifacts
of your era idealistic,
      heavier, even your disposables
            seemingly more permanent but now
                  shattered to shards, splintered and bent
to intricate lace of rust.

      Look: the blown television tubes that
            brought the farce of *Father Knows Best*
                  rest next to those faithful chewers,
your molars, and the front teeth
      you worked so hard to grow
            when you were still a child,
                  the ones knocked loose

when he pushed you down the stairs,
          they are there too. But because landfills
                    can be a place for cut grass and garden
                              slop, I also see your teeth bound by
a sweeter rot, netted into veins
          of wet leaves that remember
                    spring, mulched into bulbs
                              of spent iris, those tall, old-fashioned
ladies that while appearing
          used up and gone from
                    this world always

come back.

Fanny Says She Got Saved

Now, you listen here, fucker. I won't hear no blasphemous talk of Jesus. That old uncle of yours is Italian and married into the family and don't believe like we do, so don't pay him no mind. Now, I was saved in Bowling Green, off Cemetery Pike Road—baptized the way Jesus was, in a river—Barren Creek River. That wasn't too long after I made some money off a the church. . . . See, they paid you three cents for memorizing a verse, and so I memorized one: *And God said, let there be light.* I bought a Snickers and saved a penny donation for the revival. Yes, I'd go every time; we liked to listen to the piano and the woman with the tambourine. . . . My first cousin, Elizabeth Harris, now she never was quite right in the head, but somehow I just a listened to her, and I let her take me up to the altar that night, and I never would let anybody else take me up there.

Fanny Linguistics: Nickole

What people don't know about my name
is that my grandmother gave me that "k"
                    —my very own unexpected
consonant—
                    those two strong arms and two strong legs,
that broom-handle spine—
                    that letter about no one with a name
same as mine has.

A mis-
          spelling, really—
                    the same botched phonetics of all her
girls' names,
          misspelled but fancy

as chandeliers—*Latonna Lee, Candies La Rayne, Lesi Annett*
          —names that know never to drink
          lemon water from a silver fingerbowl

but names that can be bobbed with a "y"
          and cheerlead.

Now, she called me *Koey*, so don't expect me to respond
to the first nasal tone of my name
          but the harsher   cough

that follows, that typo tambourined
from the back of the throat. I'll answer to *cold* & *coal* & *coke*, sometimes
          even hear that sound as a scoop of *coco*, something dry

from the tin, but warmed with a little sugar and milk, a name snowing
          while it's safe inside.

Fanny Says How to Make Potato Salad

Alright now. What you got to do is get some potatoes, I used to buy them big bags of Idaho potatoes, and you need to wursh them real good and boil them whole. Now, you know how your mama cooks, like this—*plom, plom, plom*—so just drop those fuckers in the water and don't worry about them till they get soft enough to just peel with your thumbs, but not too soft, cause we're making salad here, not mashed potatoes.

So then you've got to get you one stalk a celery, the whole thing now, and peel back them big strings, cause nobody wants to have to pick their teeth while they trying to smile at you telling you your salad's any good. And chop up that celery, and then you do the same to one green pepper, not the green onion, now, but the pepper, round-like and overpriced in the grocery store.

Boil and chop you four eggs. Also you need you about six a them sweet pickles I love so much at Thanksgiving on the Lazy Susan. You can chop them up, or if you want, you can use a bit of that canned pickle relish your uncle always slopped on them nasty-ass hot dogs of his.

Also add one onion, chopped, and try to use a white one, especially them good old Vidalia onions, they not nearly as strong as the yella. Besides, you don't want to blow nobody out with your breath.

You need one a them big bowls, you know, about this big around, and mix it all real good with your hands. Now you know you got to have a little salt and pepper, and three tablespoons or so a mayonnaise, or if you want to make it the real way I used to like, use Miracle Whip. Now, be careful now with that mayo, make sure that shit's fresh or you'll ruin the whole batch and have everybody in the house running to the bathroom. Also add in about the same amount a plain yella mustard. You know, the kind that's yella as a gourd and comes in one a them round bottles.

While you're mixing it with your hands, bring the bottom to the top. You might even want to add a jar a pimentos for color. Now, be sure and take a bite in your mouth before you serve it—it's gotta have a little wang in it, it can't be dull. If it is, add a little bit a sugar or vinegar to it.

Cover it up and let it sit in the fridge for one hour. It should be enough to last you three or four nights, and of course, if your husband's coming home, you might want to make it all pretty by putting it all on top a some lettuce leaves and dusting it with a little a that paprika.

Fanny Linguistics: Superstition

In Fanny's house, there were ways of killing
someone by walking alone: I could step over
my youngest uncle sprawled watching TV,
could step over his boy heart or leg or arm—
it wouldn't matter which—because *unless you step back*
over him, right quick, by morning he'll be
gone.

Same goes for a bird let in the house—a sparrow
in the laundry room had wings
of the Great Scythe, and a black crow
tangled in the living room curtains could well wipe
the whole family out. And should you dream
of losing your teeth—that meant death
coming sure as an owl shits
tiny bones of mice in the middle of the night;
it was a full-on omen, start baking
the funeral casseroles now.

Funny, all that hoo-doo about dying with no intent
to remember the dead—how Fanny hated photographs:
I don't take pictures, she said. *It just makes me sad,*
and if anything ever did happen
to one of the kids, I don't want to be left
staring at their face.

The Dead

It was the ones no one remembered who pulled at me.
—Dorothy Allison

So tell me, who remembers Topa, her daddy, his face marked with smallpox
or his two sisters, *one that died one day, the otheren the next?*

Who remembers quarantined houses marked with a red card, the brain
fevers and blood fluxes, or the uncle who found a rafter in the tobacco barn

for his neck? And wasn't there a second cousin
who phoned his brother before making a confetti

of his own brains? Or that other young uncle—*a good-looking
son of a bitch*—who, face-down in the river, took mud

into his handsome lungs? Or the babies—Jesus, always the babies—
drowned in washtubs or bit by brown recluse, or Claire, a girl born

four months early, small enough to crib in a shoebox
who thrived, but her brother—*full-term, healthy as a horse*—

who was sleeping sound on his second day when he
just died?

And who remembers Yael but me, that girl with the name so pretty
I could taste the syllables—*Yah Elle*—

and called her again and again? She was only
seven, her blood a sandstorm of cells, at war with itself.

Or my soft-spoken cousin, that kid
surfer who thought he could crush time-

release pain killers with his teeth and
live? Does anyone remember how impossible

death seemed in Florida, how like a sun-scorched
fern his hands curled, two black fiddleheads, the foam at his mouth

when all his chickenshit friends left him
for dead? On the way to his funeral, Fanny got after us for wearing black:

All you young girls always wearing dark, dark, dark, she said. *You need to put on a bright
and purdy color, something that don't make you look so depressed all the fucking time.*

We laughed, reminded her where we were going, but who can say
her fussing was a joke—her amnesia seemed

fender-struck, a switch flipped
off inside a woman *who couldn't take no more.*

Later that day we walked to church under mangroves swarmed
with the bright green fluster of wild parakeets.

I can't say I remember much more than my aunt, how she looked
up into the trees, said, *Oh, little birds, don't you know?*

And the birds, briskly chittering back, answered her:
No.

Fanny Linguistics: Birdsong

Ornithologists claim even birds chirp with
dialects, singing the same syrinx tune
          bluegrass in one region,
          subway jazz in another,

and I imagine a jay—fierce blue mother
          cawing from the trees—
          up north
                    clearing her throat,
                    a librarian whisper of
                    Quiet, son, please
          but here
                    a hot-scald blister of
                    Boy, shut your mouth.

Fanny would be tickled by that,
          she'd say again
          there wasn't an animal she'd tolerate
          except a bird,
how she never did like puppies or kittens or nothing.

Just birds, she'd say, then:

When I was little, we didn't have no running water
so used to pull our britches down
and pee on the ground then pull them up again
to squat and look at the little chicks.

She might sip her Pepsi, squint
like she was sighting a rifle, add,

See, it was such a different time; necessity meant you ate
even the little things you loved. Aunt Lonni, she had chickens,
and she killed hers.

Fanny Says She Learned to Throw the First Stone

Aunt Lonni, sweet Addeline, her husband was cheating on her with a woman named Edna. Now, I never will forget it. . . . I saw that woman's car, it was sky blue, and back then, those roads, Koey, they were made out of big rocks, and I just stopped and picked up one and then another and threw em . . . like this . . . and well, let me tell you, I tore the back of her car and that window *all* to pieces.

And Aunt Lonni, she knew all about Edna—even knew her name—but she said, *Fanny, now you shouldn't do that, don't you dare,* but all the while she was just a loving it and covering her mouth and a laughing.

And when my uncle saw me, he said, *I'm a gonna kill you,* but I said, *I'm a gonna sue you for all that money you owe me.* See, he had promised me ten cents to carry in five loads of wood, and by the time I got to the last load, he was already halfway to town. . . . See, he would stay gone all weekend.

He had three kids by that mistress.

Hettie

was the name she called us, and what she meant was clumsy,
graceless, *all assholes and elbows tripping up the steps*, then laying eyes on me, saying,
Well, I don't figure that child's ever gonna learn to ride that bicycle,
how long she gonna perch stone-still on that thing, propped on the kickstand?
I bet Hettie here knows she's bound to bite the dust before she even leaves the drive.

Hettie, as in:
Well, Hettie, you done broke your grandmama's crystal bowl
in a thousand pieces, meaning, *you ain't never had a summer in all your live-*
long life without scabbed knees, meaning absentminded, plum-bruised,
the side of my leg catching corners, or meaning, as a book put it,
the absence of pleasure makes one clumsy, or in another text, *a person post-*
trauma can disassociate, quit paying attention, survive the crash
soft-limbed, like a drunk.

Hehhh-Teeee, hollered two-tone,
mountain-style, a come-and-get-it supper bell,
at times meaning you did something off-kilter, singed with violence,
as in, *Well, Hettie, whatever you did to that boyfriend of yours made him mad*
as a hornet, looks like he plum wore out the side of his van with his fist,
or, *Well, Hettie, I can't believe you just blew the head clear off*
your doll with that firecracker. Because, *Yes, Hettie, you really did it this time,*
meaning, *at least you didn't*
kill nobody.

There was a Hettie once,
a *real* Hettie, way back in the family,
but *she was crazy as a loon, spent her whole life at Central State with*
her finger up inside her trying to grab men's things. Hettie the nymphomaniac,
the queen masturbator, the gal that at a picnic *grabbed Monroe's*
thing, the one *that would fuck a snake if it didn't*
have a head on it. Hettie, imagined with wild red hair and mosquito-pocked legs,
the fists of her raw knees peeking out from under her tie-back hospital gown.

Hettie, the only woman we knew who *wanted it,*
who wouldn't say

I'd rather
toothbrush the kitchen floor on my hands and knees,
wouldn't say, *I'd just as soon set my hair on fire,* wouldn't whisper,
I counted each and every rose on the wallpaper before he was through,
or *I'd rather pluck my curliest hairs out one-by-one than deal*
with him tonight, all said in half-jest, a joke hollered down from their teetering
pedestals, making the men rooster up, all said making one thing clear:
I ain't no Hettie, ain't no loosey-goosey hot-pants whore.

But I can't help
but wonder, can't help but make up something
for our Hettie, something to do with a house on stilts in the holler
and a father who took her right under the floorboards where
her mother stood, but who knows, she could have pulled her budding
breasts out for Captain Kangaroo, she could have rubbed herself
raw on the old tweed couch, a tarpaper ten-cent
trick, for all we know—

which is nothing,
which is Hettie is the name Fanny called us, and if you're not
a *Hettie* then you're hands-and-knees down scrubbing the floor, that if
what happened to you doesn't make you one way, it will make you
another—that you won't exist at all or you'll be
too much—either tripping up the porch steps
to tell Mama what happened
or crawling under them to take
more, all the while wanting
to hide, hot
with a match
catching underneath
the old wood
planks.

Fanny Says How to Be a Lady

1. Never tell your age. If under cardiac arrest and the ambulance comes, the paramedic will ask lots of questions—the city you live in, the president, your last name. Answer him best you can, but if he asks the year you were born, say, *You're the doctor here. If you're so fucking smart, why don't you tell me how old I am?*

2. Watch your reputation close. Remember, if you lie down with dogs, you'll come up with fleas, and no man will buy a cow if he gets the milk for free. Now, if you need a husband, put on a pair of pants—tight now, so it shows your rump—and get a little chain to walk that dog. Go on to that fire station and walk past. Now those firemen are gonna notice you and whoop and holler, but you don't pay them no mind, you just keep walking with your head held high. By the fourth or fifth time you walk past, one of them's gonna say, *Well, I'm going outside to talk to that ho . . .* and that's just what he'll say . . . but I'm sure he'll learn right different, soon enough. And then? It'd be all she wrote.

3. Take it easy, keep your feet up, and don't carry nothing heavy unless you want your uterus to fall out on the hot sidewalk. And if you lift weights, you'll lose your perky breasts, *you won't be left with a tiddy one*; trust your grandma, stay away from the gym, cause like I say, *I don't believe in exercise, no, not one bit.*

4. Speaking of your tiddies, once you lose them, you can't get them back. Wear a brassiere with a good wire day and night, even to sleep, and don't let no baby nurse you. If you do, they'll deflate into two bananas. Then what will you do? Ain't a thing wrong with bottle-feeding—look at you, raised up on formula from day one, and you seem to be alright.

5. Steer clear of places where common people go. Public pools ain't nothing but a sea of hot piss, and if you're forced to drink in a restaurant, you ask for a straw, because Lord knows where that cup has been.

6. Don't fool with a boy with no home training. If he pulls in front of the house and lays on the horn, don't you answer. You ain't no whore, he needs to come to the front door proper and knock. And when you get to his car, Grandma will be watching to see if he opens the passenger side. If not, you stand still, let him jump in alone . . . soon enough,

he'll notice you're not in the car and come around to open your door. I mean it: I'll be watching, and if you so much as touch that handle, I'm coming out to whup your ass. A man will respect you once you've earned it. Start a puppy early, and he won't pull the leash.

7. Don't answer the phone, specially if a boy you like is calling. I don't care if you're picking your toes and watching *The Flintstones* on a Friday night, you let Grandma answer. I'll tell him, *No, she's not here, she went down to Miami with a few girlfriends and never came back.* When he sees you, you got to pretend now—*Oh, we had such a good time. We played volleyball and got a tan.* That will keep him from taking you for granted, for waiting so long to call, thinking you'd always be there, waiting around.

8. People mostly see what you say. Now, if you've got a crooked nose, let them know and that will be all they notice. And your feet? I know they're flat and turned in, big enough to row a canoe, but tell people and they'll think you're afflicted. Look in the mirror, girl. You're as pretty as you let yourself be; you're just fine.

9. Don't ever let folks think you're trash. Don't sit with your legs open drawing flies, don't ever let me see you drink straight from a bottle or can, and for God's sake, never serve coffee with the stirring spoon still in the cup. Wear your hair up after thirty, but never let nobody cut it off, and at suppertime, don't you dare touch the last bite. You don't want people to think you're hungry: if you enjoy somebody else's dinner, don't say thank you for *the meal*, but thank you for *such a nice time.* Don't track in through the front door unless you're company; if you're family, use the back. And if you've been drinking from the same glass for a few hours, it's greasy, get yourself a clean one, fresh from the dishwasher. Ain't no sense ever being dirty; soap don't cost a nickel, now, soap's cheap.

10. Be mean and fight for it. That's the only way it will ever come to you. Remember what Grandma tells you: People will take only what you let them, and you hold that head back and walk straight. You understand? Be mean, fight for it. Hold that head back, walk straight. You'll remember what I tell you? You'll remember, won't you?

II

Two or three things I know for sure, and one of them is what it means to have no loved version of your life but the one you make.

—Dorothy Allison

Clorox

1.

A noun,
        as in a commercial disinfecting agent,
but also a verb,
        an action to make the water grow
        teeth—tiny, crystalline, color-eating teeth—

making the water
        capable, bringing red
        to its knees:
your oxblood tee now the color of
nipples, your salsa-hot dress neutered
cheap carnation pink,
        all our deepest purple
        a sad, dry rot of brown.

A complete sentence might read:
        Careful now, or Fanny's gonna clorox
the shit out of your clothes; you and I know
        she burns through a bottle a week.

But more likely, you'd hear:
        Child, you looking like some trash.
        Give your grandma that dinge.
        I don't care if you ain't got a dime.
        I told you a hundred and one times—
        soap's cheap.

2.

A noun,
       but also a verb,
       as in *to clorox:*

to clorox that carny tub and toilet,
to clorox the chicken-grease backsplash and hand-smudge light switch,
as in *to clorox* the cup
       Donason drank from
       when he visited

       up from Miami
       to smoke cigarettes and
       to try not to say
       goodbye.

Even at six, I could see
       the Kaposi sarcoma
       too big for the joy
       of the violet scarf
       spangled round his neck.

He was one of the boys
       she took in,
       raised right
       alongside her own, but

when he left, she cloroxed that cup twice,
       then threw it out.

3.

A smell—
       wealth sweetened with a little zip,
       a salty tang,
       a bright chlorine rising up
       to say, *it's alright now,*
       put your babies in water wings, let them splash in,

because this ain't nothing
       like that piss-yellow swimming hole
       sick with *infantigo*, this ain't nothing like Bowling Green
       where the only time she let herself get dunked
       was to be baptized in that mudbottom river
       named Barren.

Come. This water is modern,
       this water is amnesiac
       with no memory of leathery eggs
       of cottonmouths hatching in its bank
       or catfish whiskering the
       holes below;

hell, this water can't even remember
       common spiders that once straddled its surface,
       walking impossible
       as Christ himself.

4.

An agent manufactured specifically
       to break the chemical bonds
       of color,

as in to clorox the tub white and the toilet
whiter, as in to clorox the tile white and the grout
whiter, as in to blanch a house
a hundred shades of white—

> *antique lace* walls and *cloud* trim, the unforgiving stark
> of Formica cabinets and counters, the sleepy *snow*
> sheets and shag rugs, the *bone* leather sofa and matching chairs,
> the *take-off-your-shoes-or-Fanny's-gonna-whup-your-ass*
> wall-to-wall white carpet
> white enough to put Elvis' living room
> to shame,

everything brand and spanking and new,
> everything white
> *because you know and I know other people are lazy*
> *and buy dark colors to hide*
> *dirt, but you know my house is clean by looking,*

her house white
> as a baby's bottom, white
> as the pure driven, so white she kept
> a black maid six days a week to keep it so.

Now, Bernie, she'd fuss. *We got to clorox that damn floor.*
> *Those boys clomped through here—look at those tracks*
> *right cross my clean white rug.* And so

Bernie May put down
her coffee, and without gloves,
cloroxed it all
over again.

5.

A formula genius in design—
       with high reactivity and instability
       it works quick then
       disappears,
       almost as if it had never been there
       at all.

Blow up, blow out, blow over,
       she'd say after he took
       the safety
       off his jigsaw with a hammer,
       after he tried to fix the broken head
       of a sprinkler with a hammer,
       after he ran the hood
       of his pickup through her
       carport again.

       He knocked us
       into chairs and into closets and down the stairs,
       and if you tried to stand before
       he was done, he'd knock you
       back again.

You see, me and Monroe,
       well, me and all my kids,
       we were natural:
       we'd fuss and fight and holler and make up
       by suppertime.

Ain't no sense in holding it in, and damn well ain't no sense in dragging it out again.

Reader, listen—

You've got bad water from the well?

We all do
one time or another.

Just splash a little Clorox in and wait,
        and not too long.
        This is a poison that works quick then is
        gone; this is a poison she saw fit enough
        for us, for all of us, to drink.

Fanny Says She Didn't Use to Be Afraid

I never was close to Evelyn though. She was always the good daughter, helping to sweep and helping to mop and sitting outside on the swing porch watching Bobby and Billy. But I wasn't no good. I wasn't nearly as good of a daughter. I was out, all the time, just a walkin the alleys, and if I'd see a cigarette butt on the ground this short, I'd smoke it. Mama always kept the matches over the stove, and I'd steal them. I smoked cigarettes all day long, but never did buy any, I don't know why. I guess cause I could find them and smoke them and not have to worry about no AIDS or nothin. We didn't worry about them things them days.

Fanny Linguistics: Publix Hieroglyphics

Most every day meant
a trip to the grocery,
which called for a special skill—
       reading Fanny's grocery list.

A pile of dots could be
       peas, hominy, or *pintos,*
and with a cylinder next to it,
       add: *a can of.*
A cylinder alone was
       toilet paper,
and drawn bigger meant
       paper towel.

She drew tiny boxes, tiny bags, tiny cups;
she drew
       icons of *bread, chicken, beef,*
       motion lines of *sliced, quartered, ground.*

Once, we knew
       a tangle of squiggles
       was *spaghetti,*
we were sure,
       but even with years of experience,
best not get too cocky:

when we got home, she asked what the hell
       we bought that nasty-ass pasta for.

Well, son of a bitch, she said. *Look close*
       at that list I done gave you.
See? Look here. That's no spaghetti.
       Can't you read?
          That's sauerkraut.

Fanny Linguistics: Origins

If asked about her education, she'd say,
    You mean schooling? Well, mostly
    a wooden chair—

ladder-backed, straight,
raw wood,
small, hard, hand-hewn,

pegged together
with no glue, no nails.

    She'd say,
    I'd pull my wooden chair
    up to Daddy's
    wooden chair.

    I'd ask him how to spell.

    And he'd help me spell

    until he said,
    "Frances Lee, it's time for bed now,"

    and I'd say,
    "Alright, Daddy,"

    and I pushed my little wooden chair

    up under the dark table
    and did like he said.

Crisco

1.

A brand in a can and, later, conveniently in sticks, but also a word—*crisco*—
applying to any shortening, any oil teased from its natural state to stay solid

at room temp. Used with a peppering of coffee grounds to fry chicken,
or with ice water to roll flat a pie crust, or in her cornbread, made the only right way:

with buttermilk, in a skillet cured and cast iron.

2.

Crisco, the first shortening made from plants, mostly cottonseed up from Delta
labor and heat, the first shortening entirely free of slaughter, the hog she remembered

hung upside-down, the six-inch stick knife that made an animal
flesh, the come-along jack that hoisted what was now carcass

into a cauldron of boiling water and lye, the bell scraper that teased a body from
its own bristle, teased it right out of its own skin.

3.

A Depression-Era cure-all—for ashy elbows, for rusty skates, for squeaky hinges
and cracked heels and cuticles and psoriasis and hemorrhoids and bicycle chains.

Back then, there wasn't much Mama could afford, so her mama bought Crisco for
most anything that needed attention, a bit of moisture, a dab of grease.

4.

Crisco, because Fanny says you have to wear your husband out, and sometimes
you might be counting flower petals on wallpaper, but you best pretend,

Just put a little shortening up there, she said,
he'll never know the difference.

5.

Monroe said to her once: *Fanny, what do you think a man
thinks about all day?   Beans and cornbread?*

For her, Crisco popped and pocked tiny round burns
down both arms, Crisco sizzled and melted

and started a full-on grease fire only
salt could put out.

Crisco clogged her pores and dulled the walls;
Crisco slowly filled the delicate tubes leading in and out of

Monroe's heart.

> But for now, say it is evening, the kids are outside playing
> kick the can, the floor mopped, the dishes done,
>
> she is bone-tired, ankles swollen, but he waits
> upstairs. She opens the tin, uses two fingers to slide
> a dollop in.

For My Grandmother's Feet,
Swollen Again

But for one pair of storebought boots,
    your two feet grew up barefoot
        with no idea you'd be bedridden,
            expecting for the last time at forty
your seventh child. And your sixth—
    your youngest daughter—my mother,
        would play shoe shop with a string.
            It's her favorite story: how she laced
your feet with pretend ribbon,
    pretend satin, pretend lace,
        how she tied a bow and said,
            How about this pair, Mama,

would these do? I can't say
    I was there, but the half of me
        that was round and fully formed
            nested in the mouth of her ovary,
waiting to be allowed down
    its long swan throat, and at times
        when I'm too sick to get out of bed,
            I curl the edge of a haunted sheet
between my toes to feel
    a pair of imaginary slippers
        made by a little girl who waits
            for me at the edge of my bed. This memory—

is it mine to have? My feet
    are three sizes too big, paddle feet,
        unpolished, feet that never bore
            the weight of child and might never

will. But still, when my body fevers,
      when I am weak, there is something
            bittersweet threading the loneliest part
                  of me, something that says, *Now,*

it's time. I've made you new shoes.
      Stand up.

Fanny Says How to Tend Babies

1. When expecting, you can smoke and tan and dye your hair, but don't you go reaching up on the clothesline: believe you me, Barbara lost Charlie the minute she reached up on the clothesline—the cord wrapped around his neck and killed him. And don't you dare straddle a bike or run or do anything too physical. If you need to stretch your fat legs, walk around the block. You'll want to hide your belly while you're out there too, so do like Grandma did and have somebody make you some pretty tops, loose now. I had one in every color—aqua, pink, and yella.

2. Ain't nothing to tending a baby once he's here. I had seven, I know. No sense in going out and getting baby magazines and all that expensive shit swinging and rocking and propping your baby up. You won't use it two seconds, and besides, it won't be no good to you in six months. Shoot fire, we used to use a dresser drawer as a crib. Use common sense—now, if you're hot, they're hot. If you're cold, they're cold. All you need for his little rashy ass is a sprinkle a cornstarch and about an inch of water to wash it in the sink.

3. Women been having babies for a hundred and one years, and you don't need no fancy doctor telling you what to do. Well, look at you: you had diarrhea and looked just like a monkey in a cage in that hospital. See, people will just let you do anything to your babies when the doctor say so . . . and there you sat, Koey, your heart was broke, just a crying your eyes out. And I was a real bitch then, I had all a that money and I just *threw* it around . . . and I said, *Lisa, here. You take the baby and wrap her up in my coat* (they had you naked as a jay bird), and I went down to the gift shop and got you a gown and a pair of booties and a big pink nursing blanket. And the doctor said, *You can't take that baby out of here,* and I said, *Just watch me.*

4. Now, listen to your grandma: when you come home from that hospital, you keep off your feet six weeks. Don't get up to do nothing but bathe and sleep and eat, and get you a little bassinet in the bedroom to keep that baby right beside you. You'll need to heal that flitter, so don't you move. When the baby sleeps, you sleep. Don't think his nap's the time to clean the house and run around. You start sweeping the floor and going to the store before your time, and mark my words, you'll liable to bleed to death.

5. Breastfeeding will ruin your tiddies, so steer clear of all them hippies that tell you what to do. Now, you don't want him to get the thrush, so make sure to clean the milk out of his mouth when his formula is done. Take some distilled water with a teaspoon of white Karo syrup and let him swallow that down. But don't use the same nipples that you use for your milk; that water bottle needs a smaller hole, less you want him to choke to death. If he gets the colic, next time put a little paregoric in his milk. That should do the trick.

6. You don't want an ugly baby now, so sleep him on his stomach; it keeps the head from getting flat in back. Because if that happens, you'll end up spending all your time rubbing circles on his head, trying to work it back into shape. If you don't believe me, take your cousin Jeremy: I done come twelve hundred miles just anticipating to see him, and Lord, if that wasn't the ugliest youngin I ever did see. And I said *it was a wonder Toni had him covered up.* . . . She said he was covered cause he was sleeping. Sleeping's ass. All I knowd was that his head was that long, and when I watched him he fell off the couch. And I said, *Toni, Toni come in here, I think your baby's dead.* . . . Well, I never was one for babysitting. And Lord. The way Toni used to rub his head to work it back into shape.

7. Get yourself some help, cause you got laundry ahead. You'll want to change that baby's sheets every single day, and wursh his clothes separate from yours—you don't want your nasty bloomers and your husband's socks bumping up against the baby's things. Use Dreft detergent. Now, you can dry the baby's things in the dryer, but everything will need to be seasoned, specially when the baby's new. Put out everything flat on the bed, set it out at least for twenty-four hours, till all the moisture is out.

8. Sterilize everything that goes in that baby's mouth. Boil the bottles and the nipples and the rattlers, and if a pacifier falls on the floor, don't let me catch you clean it off with your mouth. I mean it; I'll whup your ass. Less you want that baby sick as a dog, you throw it on the stove and boil it again.

9. After six weeks, you and the baby emerge. You might give the little fucker rice cereal then—mix one teaspoon of formula, one teaspoon of cereal. See, you want a sturdy baby, so best to get him on food soon as you can; milk babies get fat but don't have no tone. And when he's ready for more, don't waste your money on those little jars of baby food. Mash up potatoes and mash up macaroni—most any food that don't have color is fine—and when a few teeth come in, cut up a White Castle too.

10. If he gets the croup, use whiskey, honey, and lemon to break up that phlegm. Now, he'll cough and puke it up, but that's what he's supposed to do. If he starts fussing when he's teething, give him a wet rag from the freezer and a baby aspirin too.

Your husband won't help you none, and that's fine. He has his work to do. You got to give a man space. Let him mow the grass and plant the tomatoes and smoke his pipe all day long on the back porch. He'll be thinking on his day off, and you just need to keep doing what you're doing. Don't mind him at all.

Fanny Says She Wanted to See Elvis

It was his first time on the tee-vee, and all Monroe and I had was a ten-dollar radio, and I wanted to go out to Mama's and see him. And I don't think Monroe would have agreed, but I was out to here, like always, embarrassed to death to be pregnant again. But he was jealous as a dog and all pissed off cause he knew I wanted to see Elvis dance the hootchie-coo like he done. And you wouldn't believe it, but we got all the way out there, and they filmed him from here up, nothing below the belt, so you couldn't see a damn thing. Monroe was on the porch with his pipe; he wasn't studying it.

EPO

KRS 403.740 Emergency protective order.
*If, upon review of the petition, as provided for in KRS 403.735, the court determines that
the allegations contained therein indicate the presence of an immediate and present danger of
domestic violence and abuse, the court shall issue, upon proper motion, ex parte, an emergency
protective order . . .*

Forgive me. I was sixteen, hard-headed, big-haired, ready to fight.
I was newfangled, a know-it-all, a meddler with an overstuffed
carpetbag. Forgive me. I talked you into it; I took you downtown.

For saying you were silly to be afraid of traffic and parallel parking,
of meters and paperwork and the family court judge. *Fanny, we can do this*, I said
like some kind of cheerleader dumbstruck with virtue, ready to change the world.

Let me do this, I said. School was out, I had my own car, and it was easy
enough to call the pizza joint and tell a version of the truth:
I can't come in to work; I feel kinda sick.

The world *dislocated* hung on my tongue—your cabinet from its hinge, your shoulder
from your arm. For the word *grandfather* curdled in my mouth, and I thought
we could spit it out.

Forgive me. For the obscenity of your size-five house slippers up the courthouse
stairs, for the security guard, eyeing through the x-ray machine, suspicious
of all your little disco cases—one for lipstick and another for your lighter, even

your cigarette holder a gold box threatening his big-man screen. Forgive me for
the conveyor belt; it smudged your white pocketbook, and for the life of me,
we never could get it clean. Because even then I knew what I'd done—

*Oh, Fanny, I didn't realize this place would be so dirty. Who in God's name pissed
right on the wall? I wish somebody would talk to us; I wish somebody would take a rag
to that nasty Plexiglas, and here, sit on my coat, I know these hard plastic chairs are killing*

your knees. Forgive me for the hours we waited
in the ash and gum and grease, the angry men pacing angry, the women on their knees
changing diapers, babies back-flat on the cold tile floor.

Forgive me. For while we waited, I fooled with the official initials:
Elephants Pick Olives.
Elves Pursue Orchids.
Egypt Ponders Ontario.
Eggs Produce Odor.

Again, I'm so sorry:
Evelyn Punched Out.
Eve Pinched Ocher.
Edith's Pussy Opened.
Enough, Please, Ouch.
Everyone Pummeled Over.
Each Pushed Out.

Forgive me. I thought I could stomach what happened to things jerked
from their homes—jellyfish puddled to wet tissue on the shore
the same as a yellow iris cut and brought inside, how quickly the bloom

makes Kleenex of her beautiful face. You wore your hair in rollers under a scarf
wrapped so tight it looked like you were an immigrant to your own country,
a lady prepared for snow in spring, and your signature at the bottom of the form

was old-fashioned, practiced, perfectly slanted, and I mused:
*Even if she never really learned to write, she sure made certain
her signature looked good.* When the caseworker called

your married name, he insisted he talk to you alone.
Forgive me, I let him do that, I let him, and you swallowed and sweetly said,
Alrighty then, here goes.

[65]

Fanny Says at Twenty-three She Learned to Drive

So we were driving down Broadway towards Fountain Ferry in his new pickup. I was about twenty-three, with four kids and this stringy hair. And I look out the window and seen it: the most beautiful lightest green car you ever did see.

I knew Monroe had been promising me a car but wouldn't do it, and so I called Betty Sue in the morning to get the number of the dealership, and she said, *No, you can't, sister. Monroe will kill you,* and I said, *Well, it wouldn't be the first time.*

So I called and said, *Is this a salesman?* And he said, *Yes.* And I said, *Well, this is Mrs. Monroe Jackson Cox.* And well, they didn't know Monroe from Adam, but I said it just like that: *Monroe J. Cox, C-O-X,* with authority, because no one knew him, but they eventually would cause I would make him known.

I said, *Do you still have that light green car in the window?* And he said, *Yes.* And I didn't even know the name of the car or nothing but asked for it, just like that—*pale green*—and he said, *Yes.* And I said, *Good. I'd like to buy it.* And he said, *You'd like to buy it?* And I didn't ask the price or nothing but said, *Yes.*

Those were the olden days so there was no contract or nothing, and so he said, *Okay, Mrs. Cox, when would you like that delivered?* And I said, *Twelve noon,* because I knew that'd be right before Monroe got home. And they delivered the car, and I told them they had to pull it around for me to the back (see, we lived in a little old house, in Germantown), and we had steps—one, two, three—leading up to the back door, and my kitchen was right there, and the man said, *You don't want to pull it up yourself?* And I said, *No. I don't drive.*

He said, *You don't drive!?* And I said, *No, I'll learn tomorrow.* (And later, of course, I said to Monroe: *I've learned everything else with you, so you'll learn me this too.*) And the man said, *Okay,* and left the car right there.

Shortly after, Monroe came home, just a glarin at me and asked, *Whose car is that?* And I said, *It's mine.* And he said, *Give me the keys.* And I said, *Okay.* Then he looked at me square in the eyes and said, *I'm going to put some gas in it, cause I bet they didn't leave you a nickel's worth.*

And he did, and he started riding around, and he pulled up his sleeve to show his arms. He was so young and handsome then, with his strong, dark arm hanging out the window. And I know'd what he was thinking: he was thinking he was hot shit riding around in that thing, so he never said a word.

Dixie Highway

1.

Past the starting line in Louisville, Dixie's a six-lane tangle,
  used car lots made carnival—balloons and barkers, cheap
  strings of lights and triangle flags—then discount
  recliners, country kitchen oak, concrete
  ducks dressed in bonnets for your lawn, racks and racks
  of knock-off jeans, knock-off bags, and for the working man,
  manly bins of wife-beaters and white tube socks.

  Dixie is all-you-can-eat—ribeye, T-bone, sirloin—
  you pick your own piece of meat—and the buffet ends with
  soft-serve, *sprinkles in every color for the kids.*
  Here, the highway's bottomless, buy-one-get-one-
  free, *come on down to Big Tom's, we'll do ya up right,*
  until the road bends to
  girls with big tiddies and bad teeth, girls doing
  best they can at *Dixie's Trixie* and *Go-Go-Derby Gals,*

  and when we drove past, it was always
  breakfast time, the trucks still parked in those gravel lots
  looking terrible lonely
  in broad morning light.

2.

Outside town, Kentucky was all winter,
  mud wind-whipped to beige
  ice and trees brittled
  bone, the lanes blood-smeared with
  deer and stray dog,

and on walls of rock
blasted from the mountain,
limestone wept long stalactites
of frozen white.

Because my body was small, I still fell
asleep to rocking things
and dreamt to the tires'
pop n churn, pop n churn
waiting for Fanny to say,
Wake now up, Koey,
hours later when Tennessee
pines greened things up again.

Next came the long fingers
of moss haunting
Savannah's branches,
then came
orange groves, miles and miles
of fruit polka-dotting a waxy sheen.
Finally, a miracle—a wonder
like a troll doll spun
on a pencil's eraser end—growing not
out of dirt or clay or what men
tracked in on boots,
but from clean, easy-to-sweep-away sand,
a tree without *leaves* that fall
and need to be raked but *fronds*,
the kind cut and braided at church
Sunday before the capital-*S* son goes and dies
all over again.

*We'll go with Fanny, and we'll go to the beach every day, all our problems
gone,* Mama said, *because at the end of Dixie is The Florida Turnpike,
at the end of the turnpike's the sea.*

3.

We took Dixie because Dixie was made for
      a car like Fanny's, a car that preferred
      old highway, a car that wanted nothing to do with
      needless speed, a car that was built
      to coal-barge glide, owning the damn road.

It was a Cadillac, her Eldorado, a car impossibly
      long with impossible fins, white and waxed and gassed
      ready-chrome-go, the interior kid glove in Atomic Red,
      a climate-controlled bomb shelter, an escape hatch,
      an automobile called home.

      The factory mats were replaced with white shag rugs,
      and because I was a child, I was allowed to be the little animal
      I was, curled up and hiding in that woolen nest
      behind the driver's seat. Up front, my matriarchal line
      laughed and cussed and flicked so many cigarettes

we were our own comet,
tiny red stars sparking down that road.

4.

Dixie starts in burning cold, in gas stations
      where you have to ask for the bathroom key
      and the man hands you one chained to a hubcap that opens
      the kind of toilet Mama and Fanny say not to touch
      with a ten-foot pole.

      They suspend me over, my arms hooked
      around each of their necks and their arms holding
      my legs. I am a little girl made cable car, a cloud high above,

I am a giggle of weightlessness until Fanny says,
Enough now, pee.

Later, bathrooms don't get any cleaner, but each state
      has treasure to sell—in Tennessee, it's homemade
      lemon drops and cast iron to shape cornbread
      into little fish; in Georgia, it's billboards
      for *Pecans, Peanuts, Peaches* every five miles
      though all we buy is a bologna sandwich
      that gives Mama the shits.

      Across the final line, it's saltwater taffy
      in every *Miami Vice* shade, and Roy Rogers welcomes
      weary travelers with stale biscuits and sticky showers
      and Pac-Man machines. Mama gives me some quarters,
      whispers,

You see? I knew it. Even the rest
stops are better, everything's getting so green and warm and clean.

5.

How many times did we make the trip,
      Kentucky to Florida and back? So many
      I can honestly say maybe that long tar-patch highway
      is where I was raised.

It was a move we made whenever we could, more times
      than I care to count; it was a chance to leave
      behind the men and the cold; it was a long stretch
      with Howard Johnsons in between.
      Ho-Jo's is the only place clean enough to sleep, Fanny said,
      and once my weary drivers drifted off,

I'd sneak out to the hotel pool, slip under
        the surface, hold my breath,
        open my eyes to the blue lit from within.
        Amniotic, a mermaid then, a girl with nothing
        but sunshine ahead, without a clue
        as far as we got, wherever we went,
        there we would find
        ourselves, there we would still be.

Fanny Linguistics: How to Say What You Mean

If angry, simple—say, *That really pisses me off.* But just frustrated? *That burns me up.* Or if that lawyer is after you and he's *all bent out of shape,* you might decide not to pick up the phone, *cause the more you stir shit, the more it stinks.*

If your daughter finally did something right, like fix the cable box, say, *Shoot fire, bout time,* or you may want to give encouragement (you want her to hook up your VCR too) so snap your fingers, exclaim, *Handle it, Roy! Handle it!*

If someone tries to deceive you—a car dealer, rolling the Caddy's odometer back, or your granddaughter, blaming a dent in that new car on a mango that fell green from your tree—say, *Don't you piss on my head and tell me it's raining.*

If winter, leave one window open, because you can't stand being closed in, but make sure to fuss—*It's cold as a witch's tiddy,* and if below zero, the witch should be *in a metal bra.* If hot, you're flashing, which happens most year-round, it will likely be *hot as a dick, hot as piss, somebody get me a fresh Pepsi, crank up the air, quick.*

If hungry, this one's easy—*I'm bout to starve*—but if really hungry, add *to death* or *my ass off.* After two bowls of pinto beans and cornbread with green onion and sliced tomato and Frank's Red Hot, you're full, ask for your Tums, make a metaphor of your bloat to *a tick, high up on a hog, about to pop.*

If a lamp's expensive, say, *Shew, that's high,* and use the card, but if you could never afford it, not in a million years, that lamp's *as high as a cat's back.* Say, *You can keep your money, I won't let the back of your door hit me in the ass.*

If a girl's got pocked skin, buck teeth, and stringy hair, say *God bless her,* but if she's gone off and given head to every boy in the eleventh grade, the whore's heart might be *pea-picking, little,* or worse—both—as in, *God bless her little, pea-pickin heart.*

Now, if something real sad happens to the lady next door—the cancer took over, there's nothing left the doctor can cut away—say, *Ain't that a cotton-pickin shame,* but if her husband's running around while she's pumped with chemo, close the door, talk only in a whisper, even if no one else is in the whole house. Start the conversation with *I ain't one to say nothing, but you wouldn't believe;* end with *We better not say nothing, no, not a word.*

If you're the one brought low because that neighbor is your sister and you heard what's in her tumor-blocked bowels has started to come out of her mouth, *It ain't worth going into,* there's nothing to say. Best to make the girls ammonia the chandelier and fluff the couch pillows and brush the shag rugs and windex the mirrored backsplash and take all the just-cleaned crystal down to clean again—*This house is filthy. We ain't discussing it. Now, leave me be. Hey, I bet there's something good on the tee-vee. Don't give me no shit now, really. Don't you know Grandma's had enough—enough of tears?*

Pheno

as in *barbital*, as in *Luminal*, as in an injection
gone wrong that stopped the apricot hearts
of fifty institutionalized children
before the second war. Pheno—as in a barbiturate,
designed to depress, to hypnotize a seizure with the static
of its blank screen, pills like snowflakes to slow
the body's quick ticking to a single, white
note that's not happy, exactly,
but too leveled to care.

        Pheno, as in the quack days when a dentist
        diagnosed gum disease and convinced her
        to have every tooth jerked out of her
        pretty face before she hit thirty-six, as in the quack days
        when she opened her legs for a
        douche singed with Lysol to keep herself
        fresh, back when folks died of ptomaine poisoning
from punctured cans and when cigarettes assisted safe delivery—
        smoking being a safe way to keep the baby from being
        too big to birth.

Used before the FDA and never
formally cleared, Pheno is a renegade drug,
a cowboy hee-hawing outside town, not giving
a good God-damn, so it makes sense
for forty years she popped them
whenever she felt frayed—*Koey, I'm a wreck.*
Could you go get Grandma her nerve pills?

        Pheno, because some things Monroe did right—
        You can take the medicine, Fanny, he said,
        but no wife of mine's getting shocked.

This was when women didn't get depressed or upset
but had *full-on nervous breakdowns*, and for that, applied
warm gel to both temples and enough voltage

to make a bad thought into a small, wild
canary about to land before—*bye-bye, birdie*—it just
flew off.

Pheno, pronounced *Fee-No*, a good name
for a horse, a twitchy filly ridden
by an 89-pound jockey in pink and green silks,
a smart little switch in his hand. Watch her
come down the inside line, she's a beauty,
every bit as fast as the boys, she's making a run
for the roses until the mud catches her deep
stride, snaps her femur, and from the stands
you watch them put her down,
a thing gone from majesty
to dog food, right there
on the track.

All bets off, you cross Central from Churchill Downs,
find Granger's Pharmacy, the only place that will still
fill a prescription that went out with Technicolor film.

Behind a bookie board soda fountain is Mr. Granger—
he expects you, he knows why you've come.
He has the yellow bottle waiting and never charges you a dime.

If this is drug-running, you don't care: you always do
as she says. Every month, you pick it up, package it,
and mail it priority to her home on the Florida coast.

Pheno, a drug known to work different on
the old, making the elderly hyperactive, restless,

unable to sleep, up at three in the morning
wondering who stole her pretty aqua hand towels
and that new yellow bowl, accusing her son
of trying to kill her by bringing home
a clearance picking of culls—grainy tomatoes
and chicken black to the bone.

Pheno—as in *her stash of*—hundreds of pills
squirreled away in the bottom dresser drawer
she couldn't bend down to reach no more.

By then she was so sick she was sucking rock salt
off pretzels and throwing the rest in the trash—
An iron deficiency, someone said. *A loss of blood.*

It was then I held the bottles in my hand,
wondered how many
I could swallow down before I knew
what it felt like to be her, before I could
quell this sorrow out smooth as
her satin quilt.

She woke then and did something she hardly ever did:
she said my full name. *Nickole? Nickole? Where are you?*
Well, okay. I was just making sure
you didn't go.

Grandma needs you here; I couldn't see you
down on the floor; I wasn't sure where you was.

I put the pills back,
closed the drawer, turned out her bedroom light,
said, *I'm so sorry, Fanny; I'm right here. Goodnight.*

Fanny Says She Made Him Feel Better

Monroe and I, well, we used to have a lotta fun. We'd sneak off, do it under a tree in the countryside. And we'd sneak off while the girls finished up dinner and diddle in the back of the Chevrolet, and he'd say, *Fanny, I dare you*, and I'd say, *Monroe, don't you dare me*, and we'd giggle and hide on the side of the road somewheres. . . . And it was half the fun of it, really, sneaking. And I tell you, we all just about worn our husbands out. I done it a thousand times pretending. And he'd say, *Now, you had a good time last night?* And I'd say, *Yeeeahh.*

But Monroe, after his heart, just couldn't no more. And the nurse came in, and I was sitting on the foot of his bed, and she asked us, *How many times do you have sex?* And Monroe, well, he got so embarrassed, his face was as red as on that Pepsi can there, and well, just like he always does when he got embarrassed like that, he says, *Ask her.* And I coulda just about killed him, but I said, *Oh, about four times a week,* and he sat up, just a grinning like a motherfucker.

How to Dress like Fanny

Don't carry a *purse* but a *pocketbook,* and underneath
don't wear a *bra* and *panties*
but a push-up Frederick's of Hollywood *brassiere*
and a pair of *bloomers*—nylon, always white, pulled up
as far as bloomers can possibly go.

For your shoes, two options: should you need to go shopping
or get your pressure checked, lace up a pair of white Keds.
Otherwise, it's house shoes, dust-pink slippers
curled from the dryer into tiny, warm cups for your feet.

Now, every day, every single day, wear the exact same top:
a businessman's short-sleeve, white. Buy three dozen of them
three sizes too big, cut the collars off, have them bleached bright,
starched twice, and no sense in clasping more than two

buttons at the top unless you're going out—*Grandma's got to
breathe.* These are your *button-downs,* the only thing worth
hanging in your closet, and the only kind of shirt
in thirty years you've worn since you got home,

*pulled that girdle and them stockings off,
them high heels too—all that shit—and first put on
one a Monroe's shirts.* It was *right comfortable,* Fanny said,
I never wanted to wear nothing else since.

The other half of you isn't covered with *pants*
and sure as hell don't mess with a *skirt* but pulls on
fluffies—soft cotton sweats, rolled up, with all the elastic
ripped out, *cause Skinny Fanny ain't so skinny*

no more. Now, you were young once, you remember
being a kid in *britches,* a pretty thing in *capris,* and grown,
on Sunday, you wore *slacks* to Pleasant Grove, that same church
where we grieved your body that had died 1,046 miles away.

The pastor couldn't remember much—it had been so long
since you sat fanning in the pew—but he could tell
the story of Fanny in pants, *back when that's just not
what women were allowed to do.* Your slacks were pleated,

pressed with a crease, camel-hair, and those slacks
strolled towards the altar not because you were one
for women's rights or your husband built that church
with his own hands back in '63, but *Baptists be damned,
them slacks just felt good.*

Fanny Says I Need to Keep Warm

Shit. I didn't mind the cold weather in Kentucky. Not one bit. I'd just put on my false eyelashes and get cleaned up. I had my car in a garage, so not one drop a rain hit me as I was stepping from my house to my car. I'd just get myself dressed and go shopping, and I didn't mind the weather one bit.

Now, what you need to do when you wake up in the morning is set your oven about 400 degrees. Open the door and it will heat up your kitchen in no time. That's what I used to do early in the morning when I was making my coffee. I'd make my coffee and crank that heat up and I'd sit in a straight-backed chair (I don't know why I could always sit in a straight-backed chair. . . . People would ask me *Fanny, how you do that?* and I would say *I don't know, it's just so comfortable for me*), and so I'd open the oven door and prop my feet up on it and sit and read all morning. . . . I really did enjoy it, and sometimes I'd be there all day, just as toasty as can be.

Fuck those space heaters though—before you know it, you'll burn your whole house down with one a those things. Your Uncle Butchie wants to know: *Is it a kerosene heater?* Well, it better not be. You'll asphyxiate yourself with one of those. And make sure to keep it away from your bed too; you won't be nothing but a pile a ashes and a puddle a grease by morning time. Promise me you keep it away from the bed now?

Well, I know I'm a runnin up your phone bill. I'll talk to you later, baby. Grandma loves you too.

III

People are trapped in history, and history is trapped in them.
—James Baldwin

A Genealogy of the Word

1.

Saying "the n-word" is a cop-out, robbing
       history of its essential
       grit, faked out, vaguely
       Pentecostal, pleated and ironed stiff,
       like *dagnabbit* and *bullfish* and *flip it to dip*.

Fanny was authoritative
       with her cussing, unabashed
       with *cocksucker* and *fucker* and *dick*.

Most times, I'd laugh, pour her a fresh Pepsi
       or do whatever else she was barking out,
       but that word made me hot
       with shame; out of her mouth

it was visible, a skidmark, a shit
       stain.

2.

Bernie May came to the house regular
as the mail: she'd take a hair brush
to the shag rugs then to my ratty head;
she'd Comet the toilets minty blue then squeak-clean
mirrored tables, mirrored counters, mirrored walls,
sometimes catching a glimpse of her dark
skin in Fanny's white rooms. She'd flour up cold chops
for popping-hot lard then ice
green onions for the day's bean soup;

she'd make a walking path for the clean
white floors by laying down
clean white sheets. And always, before the day was

through, she'd put on a pot of coffee and read
the paper with Fanny, always finding news
of some girl getting raped, cut into a million pieces,
and tossed in the canal for the fish
to eat. She'd make sure to read every single word,
out loud, doing her best to terrify some sense
into my head, because, besides a string bikini,
I wore nothing
other than scrunchie socks to protect my feet
from hot sand. There was no getting past those two;
before I could head down to the beach, I had to cross

my heart and say: *No, Bernie. No, Fanny, no, ma'am.*
I swear my hand I'll be careful. I won't let myself
get raped.

3.

Sometimes, Bernie'd stop long enough to set up
the joke, asking, *Mrs. Cox, now say again*
what would you do if your blonde grandchild here
fell in love with a black man
like my cousin Tyrone?

Fanny'd reach into her roller bowl, pull out her gun.
She'd point it at my face.
If she was with a nigger man, I'd have to kill her.
A purdy girl like her can't get a white man?

Then Fanny'd put the gun
down, and they'd both laugh
and laugh.

Half the fun for them was to see me
jump off the couch and stomp down
the hall, but what they didn't know
was I knew Fanny'd never hurt me,
no. It was never the gun that made me
flinch.

4.

The gun—brought back from the war,
        the second, though by whom no one
        would say—was greased to an assassin's
        sheen, the sweet char of gun oil
        cool, slippery to touch.

She kept it buried
        in her roller bowl, a popcorn bowl
        pink and plastic, chock full of granny
        things: hard little cannons
        of hair rollers the same color pink,
        bobby pins, dentures, cold
        cream, metal nail files, false
        lashes, pills, safety pins,
        those silver, spring-loaded
        alligator clips
        women used to use
        to set finger waves.

With quickness, she'd noodle her hand
        under it all, fishing

from the bowl-bottom
grit of tobacco flakes and crumbled
blush; she'd finger
a few stray bullets
then wrap her palm around
its handle,
pulling it up with a force
necessary to hold on to a live thing
that's never once had
its safety on.

5.

I want to blame
  fear, blame poverty, blame
  stories back from a time
  when her daddy put
  butter in coffee, penny days
  when there wasn't a chicken fat enough
  for anybody to eat, when the hills hissed
  cottonmouth stories of a schoolteacher
  raped in the fields.

What I don't want to say is
  the corn was high and hissed too,
  that the man caught there
  was shot
  in the back
  four times

and *still,* Fanny said,
  that nigger lived.

6.

Close to death, Fanny grew more and more
afraid, and every night I couldn't get the blinds closed
tight enough: *They're always looking in at me,*
you know. And I can't walk, Koey, so I can't be
too careful.

We got all these Puerto Ricans and Brazilians
and niggers down here in Florida. The condo complex
is full of them; the boys keep tapping on my window;
they're liable to come in and slit our throats.

And your Uncle Butch wouldn't be no help, neither.
He's done gone to the track today, and he's just about
two sheets to the wind. They'd slit his throat too,
no problem. And after that they'd rape you,
put a dick in you that long and you'd wished
you was dead.

She also told me if I didn't lock the door that night
iguanas would waltz right in the condo and do
the same thing, crawl up between my legs,
until, she said, *you wished*
you was dead.

7.

That summer, a woman stops me in the hall.
There have been some complaints, she says.
The elderly woman in there. Is she your mother?

Well, she's been waving a gun at the boys going past her
window; she claims she'll shoot them dead.
What on earth do you think we should do?

I tell her the only thing I know to say:
I suggest you duck and get the hell out of her way.

8.

When Monroe was alive, he was her
　　　fist, he was her gun.
　　　They used to make splintered,
　　　giggling love in the woods:

We'd sneak off, do it under a tree.
And I said, "Monroe, somebody's gonna catch us."
And that was half the fun . . . and I said, "What if a big nigger
comes up here and gets me?" and he said,
"Ain't nobody gonna get you now that I'm here."

This was the same fist who beat
　　　his daughter for letting a black boy
　　　ride her bicycle.

His name was Rodney, Mama said. *Was it Rodney?*
Either way, he wanted to ride my bike around the block,
said he ain't never seen such purdy streamers
on a pair of handlebars in his whole life.

Mama couldn't recall if the bike was blue,
　　　but if it was, she was beaten
　　　the same color.

9.

My grandfather, the same man who grew
　　　old and celebrated living

through his fourth open heart
by selling off all but one
of the family cemetery plots
to give money to a young girl
grinning like a fool inside
his brand-new four-door, four-wheel-drive
shining white pickup.

The girl was my age, light-skinned.

Fanny said, *You know he was driving*
   almost a thousand miles every month
   to give her $900 out a his Social Security check?

   And bad as his heart was, all she ever coulda done
   was rub his old head and scratch his back.
   Bernie May gave me a name for her—a digger—
   that nigger girl.

10.

The summer of bedpans and sponge baths
and a well-oiled gun, the television was incessant,
kept on to keep out what was bound
to happen next. Fanny flipped to the sports channel:
Now that Tiger, they just hate him
out on the golf course. And I just love that nigger.

                    I want to say she loved Bernie, but she often counted
                         the bath towels after she was gone.

I just love that nigger. He done beat their ass on the golf course
and so they've got to shake his hand, and you know it's just killing 'em,
having to do that, but they got no choice. They got *to be polite and*
shake his hand and smile all big when you know it's just killing them inside.

[91]

I want to say she loved Bernie, but I wasn't allowed

in her part of town.

I just love that nigger. And I knew that little white girl he was with
wouldn't stick around long. I seen her run out on the golf course,
just a waving and screaming Tiger! Tiger! Tiger!
and I knew right then he wouldn't have nothing to do with her.
You just don't do that. And I'm sure he was out all day playing—nine to ten hours
on his feet—and came home to her wanting to go out. I don't think so.

I want to say she loved Bernie, but I wasn't allowed

to drive her home.

You know, I never went nowhere without my husband.
I got invited to one a those—Koey, what you call them plastic bowls
with the lids that snap on top? Tupperware. Yes—tupperware parties—
and Monroe looked over at me and said, "Where you think you're going?
I don't think so."

And I didn't neither. And I sure was glad I didn't when I had to wake up
at six the next morning with seven kids. No, I didn't go nowhere
without Monroe. And Tiger ain't putting up with that shit neither.

I want to say she loved Bernie, but she never

trusted her with Monroe.

11.

Sometimes, we reclaim words, make them
our own. *Dyke*, for example.
Say it: *dyke, dyke, dyke,*
        dyke, dyke, dyke, dyke.

Say it enough times, and it's a spoke
disappearing on a fast bike,
something to blow your hair back.

But if we say this word over and over, can we make it
change? *Nigger, nigger, nigger, nigger,*
              nigger, nigger, nigger, nigger, nigger,
                    nigger, nigger, nigger, nigger, nigger.

You see? It's immune, still a backhanded, redneck,
spitwad crack. It's mule stubborn, deeply
set, the only word I know not up to
this stupid-ass trick.

12.

There was one plot left
when my grandfather died,

so when Fanny's time
came, there was no room for her,

no way to bury her next to her mother,
no family earth left for her bones.

We had her cremated, and at his feet,
set her a simple stone.

I doubt Grandfather's girlfriend
knew where her sweetheart's money

came from, but if she did,
what would she buy? The bitch

in me sees a gaudy chain with her
name scripted in gold, a pair of acrylic

heels too tall to tramp her
around the block. But no. The real

sorrow—the deeper anger
harder to swallow—is for him:

he knew damn well that girl was
poor and needed cash

to live, just as Fanny needed it
to pay her doctor's bills, maybe

a few month's worth
food and rent.

13.

I doubt Grandfather's girlfriend wanted to go
        to Tupperware parties.

I don't ever remember Fanny having enough
        Tupperware to give.

Sometimes, Bernie would doggy-bag
        her dinner in foil and take it home with her
        across the tracks.

Say it: *Tupperware. Tupperware,*
        tupperware, tupperware, tupperware, tupperware,
                tupperware, tupperware, tupperware, tupperware.

See?

    Most anything,
    enough times, quits
    making sense.

14.

Sometimes, I'm afraid I will die
    an old woman blurting out
    nigger from my sour bed.

    It is not like the rational
    fear of rape, no. More
    the compulsive driving
    across that dotted white

    line, a full-on case of senile
    Tourette's, an unexplained spark
    in the orange can of gasoline
    forgotten in the shed,

    like a bullet
    that's waited too long
    for a trigger
    that decides, on its own

    just to get up and go.

15.

In second grade, I came home with a new word,
    ancestor, rolling in my mouth,
    thought of greengreen Ireland, great-grandfathers

with shields or kilts, people all the way from a poet's place
called Wales.

I had to know, I begged:
    Fanny, please, can't you tell me where we from?

Right quick, she said,
    Child, don't you worry your pretty little head bout that.
    We weren't nothing but a bunch of chicken thieves.

What I thought she meant by this was *trash*, as in
    white. Always, her joke: *Girl, you was born*
    trash, and you'll die trash. We'd laugh, and she'd say
    it again, *Yep, you trash alright. That's how you were*
    born, that's how you'll die.

Say it: *Born trash, die trash. Born trash, die trash.*
    Born trash, die trash. Born trash, die trash.
        Born, die, born, die, born, die. White,
            but trash, trash, trash, trash, trash, trash.

16.

The summer—
    that last summer—

Fanny tells me there was a woman,
        a mother
                to her mother
                        to her mother,
                              to her mother,
    count it—four generations

back—who was dark
        as a bucket of water,
an unstirred pool of black
                        left out
for sleepers who thirst
in the dead of night.

        She didn't make
much of it, just mentioned it casual
as if it were something she told
me all my life. *So there you go,*
Kunta Kinte blood, she said,
laughing softly
before turning out
her light.

17.

A slave?
In our family? Good God, Nickole, you'd believe
anything, my aunt says.
That was morphine talking.

But I swear Fanny remembered things
clear, much clearer than before,
she told way-back stories
hard as the lichen-green apples
of Kentucky, hot as the place
where she and Monroe made their first
home, an attic apartment
with a small window to the roof:

I'd sleep there with my little top
and a pair a bloomers, all sexy,

cause my legs weren't like they are
now. And I didn't take nothing
but a little blanket and pillow and wasn't nothing
above that roof and me but those stars.

She looked up to show me
just how she looked up then. I, too, looked
at that low popcorn ceiling, searching
for cloud shapes
in the mop stucco, when she said,

And then the wind picked up
over top those trees, it hit me, and it felt
so good, you wouldn't believe.

18.

Bernie May taught me how to hex
       and how to protect: in a tree right outside
       your front door, tie up bottles with string
       long enough to sway from the bough.

When the sun comes out, the spirits—
       the ghosts and memories meddling
       from another time—get distracted by all that broken
       light, all that pool-bottom beauty,
       and fly into the trap, dazzled inside.

Once, I dreamt that dark
       water, took a cool drink
       from the night to find that
       woman, that secret mother,
       arches fallen and arms strong.

She wrung the necks of chickens
and beat rugs to a thread, and when her work
was done, the bit of light
left over let her
tie bottles to a tree
that wasn't hers.

19.

Great-mother, if I ever lose my mind and call you
        nigger would you know it was because I was
        eaten alive with the cancer
        of this history, this fear working my skull up
        through my face?

Because for you, I would cross over—
        the living haunting the dead.
        Would you let me carry what's left
        of you across the river?

Not far, in Indiana, is that good earth
        where at least your bones could be set free, a cemetery
        right across the dividing line, a place where women were not
        purchased, even though they may still be cajoled into selling
        themselves to an old white man once his heart gives out
        and he's gone limp as his own flag.

20.

Forgive me. Now, I can see:
in one bottle, a tiny black knot,
not much more than a raisin—a mulatto's
umbilicus dried and broken free. In another

bottle, dumb as a housefly
and thumping against the glass, is me.

From the humid, from the stink
of old tincture, from this scratched and sugared
cage, I watch. You are bent in your garden,
on your back a colicky baby the high yellow
of rape, rounding its tiny mouth *ah, ah, ah, ah*—
to you, it's just milk-tongue all babies make, but to me,
it's those first syllables

needed, this terrible word softened, still bristling but
between family. Can you hear the hum of me,
begging, *Please, your real name*? Would you let me call you
a mother of mine? What name opens the warm mouth
of your cabin door?

Tell me, tell me how to call
you, how to conjure the sounds that bring
you here. It's me—your long-gone
grandchild, caught in this heat, in this glittering,
haint bottle in the wind.

IV

You didn't want to be no wife, Koey. You wanted to go out and see the world, and you were looking for something else. You didn't have time for a man. You don't need no husband. You need to be doing what you worked so hard all these years to do. You need to write yourself a book.

—Frances Lee Cox,
September 27, 2003

Fanny Says She Knows How Little Time Is Left

I loved green apples till I lost my teeth. I still remember them though—I was about six, and I'd climb that tree and fill my bloomers up with apples for everybody to eat and climb back down again. We ate enough of them bright green apples to make ourselves green—got so sick we could barely stand then got up the next day and went back to that tree for more. I know I told that story a hundred times, but I remember that tree and all them apples like it was here now.

No, I don't figure I'll ever taste those things again as long as I live.

For My Grandmother's Gallstones, Reconsidered

I didn't believe you when you said
        the stones from your body looked
                pulled from a treasure chest,
                        that those sad, toxic deposits
could be anything like jewels.
        No, to me they were tarry knots
                that should have been carried out
                        with stool but instead required
a scalpel to cut from you, a doctor
        who dug and found the unexpected
                tentacles, a blue tumor reaching
                        underneath.

Is despair a sin? I ask the lowly
        gallstone and find its answer
                on the Internet—a photo
                        of a small pile cleansed naturally,
looking just like you said:
        something you wouldn't believe your eyes
                until you seen it—a black diamond, a stone
                        of every color, yella and lilac and aquamarine.

When I saw that glittering I couldn't help but
        ask: Why do I always have to see beauty
                to believe? Why do I have to be shown? Despair comes
                        to me easy: I didn't need any convincing about the cancer found,
but otherwise thought you dosed,
        out of your head; I rolled my eyes,
                pressed my cup to a darker door
                        eavesdropping on death's plans instead.

It's like heaven, when I asked you
      what you thought it would be.
            You shrugged like I was downright
                  silly, asking something daft, then
                        said, *Well, it's beautiful, just like the Bible says.*

Sweet Silver

1.

You were in a bakery when you first saw it:
       hair bright as
       abalone,
       a back-lit gray kissed
       with lavender,
       a color that flashed
       like the white underside of leaves
       when strong winds flipped
       their color silver
       before a storm.

It might not have been a natural tone, but by then, you knew:
       a woman *blending in* meant
       a woman *forgettable*, and your edges
       were fading, near forty,
       a mother of six and another
       on the way,
       your smile lost to
       empty root chambers and a set of false teeth,
       your husband gone missing again,
       this time to a game of tennis
       and the instructor's little white skirt.

You bought a dozen of this, a dozen of that—
       so many mouths to feed—and before the door chime
       announced that lady's departure, you asked,
       Excuse me, what color you got on your hair?

She said, *Clairol, Sweet Silver,* and
       if anyone can name a color theirs,
       that's been your color since.

2.

This is the trick Lucille Ball could teach:
        as beauty queen, a woman is
        measured, compared to the rest,
        as sex symbol
        she ages, and unless she manages
        a spectacular suicide, she just
        disappears.

But make yourself into a funny lady,
        pull your skirt up and stomp
        barefoot in grapes, let yourself get knocked
        across the stage by a loaf of bread a mile long,
        and you're on to something,
        pile your clown red
        high, everybody loves Lucy,
        take a bow.

3.

It was an art form, really—a sculpture
        fit for Marie Antoinette,
        not a *hive* or a *bouffant* but a
        placement of silver curls
        teased to Jesus
        and set with aerosol.

Necessary tools included
        rollers, clips, perm rods,
        dense bristle brushes, rat-tail combs,
        setting lotion, and
        a hood dryer
        to bake it into place.

For the crowning touch,
       a matching Sweet Silver wiglet,
       securely pinned then blended
       like three-inch meringue
       on top.

4.

A whore's bath is what she called it—
       once she got sick, all she could do
       was stand at the sink and splash
       clean.

Her hair became
       a dandelion puff in the front,
       a shut-in's mat in the back,
       and after months of illness
       she grew roots two inches long
       in a color none of us had ever seen.

She became
       limp,
       bruised,
       pale,
       her flesh returning to
       water,
       her hair gone to
       weed.

My uncle, the one who ran a salon, he said,
       Your grandmama's just given up, that's all.
       And how do you like those lowlights in her hair?

It was a joke—

    I know, I know, I know—

but I could have

wrapped the cord of the spray nozzle

around his neck.

Instead, I smiled quiet,

stood behind her

as she gripped her walker

hard.

Her face was bent

    in the kitchen sink,

    she was white-knuckled, she was shaking,

    and eventually, she let me touch

    my fingers to her scalp.

I'm hurrying, Fanny, I know, you hurt, I know, I said.
Don't I know it, Fanny, don't I know.
Just one more minute now.
I have to work these knots out.

5.

What I wouldn't do for a lock of that hair now,

    a bright flash of

    fuck all y'all

    to braid into the ancestral

    wreath.

Can you see it?

    The intricate twists in shades of

    mouse, dishwater, ash, straw-broom—

    all the church-going,

    mannered tones of

almost-blonde,
the hair of the dead resigned to
the bleak of
autumn leaves long after
it's time to rake and
snow is on the ground.

Can you see it? There—
        at the strong base of the tree,
        that bough with seven branches forking from it, that
        carbonated platinum, that stainless Adriatic,
        the Sweet Silver of her
        last remaining threads.

Trace your finger—you might be
        surprised to find the hair
        thinner than it looked on her,
        find it has more oil,
        not enough curl,
        further proof of how
        hard she worked
        to become
        who she was.

Fanny Says She Met a Stripper Girl in the ER

There was a woman in a pink bikini in the hospital bed next to me. I knew she was there because she was a *hype, hype*—you know, like your Aunt Toni does—a panic-like, yes, that's it—*hyperventilate*. And she was hyperventilating, and she was built like a brick shithouse—she had them fake tiddies and a waist that wasn't this big and her ass was like *pow!* and she tells me that was all the clothes she had—that pink bikini—and it was barely enough to cover her nipples. I think she musta been in the burlesque, Koey, but I didn't say nothing. And she had two kids, and she musta been about your age, twenty-six, twenty-seven, and her mother was keeping them kids. And her little boy said he was afraid she was gonna die, and she told him to be quiet and stop a buggin her, and I said *phewwww*. I couldn't believe a mother could be so bad, could you? Can't be easy though, what she's got to do, stepping in those strange cars. And it's I like told her—*Honey, it's an easy ride up but a long walk down.*

Bullshit, Bullshit, Bullshit

—for Katie Mead

My friend, we die mid-
sentence. *In medias res.*
We die half-delirious in labor
reversed. You expected
poignant last words but
instead came a heap
of trash
from your mother's mouth:
bullshit, bullshit, bullshit,
she said—*bullshit*
to halos, *bullshit*
to wings, *bullshit*
to golden god mansions,
celestial beasts sharp-fingering
bullshit harp strings.

                                        Because of this, I want
                                                  to say I was once
                            in a car with another car a sliver-
                                        second from severing
                                        my throat. What I remember
                                                  most is my glorious
                                                  last thoughts
                                        would have been a dark
                            green dress, something in velvet,
                                        something exotic,
                                        a tad racy, with a slit
                                                  to reveal
                            my sides just so, but *really now,*
                                        what shoes would I wear?

Because of this, let me
tell you
a true story turned sad

joke: a woman has gone
the color of shadow
on snow, bloated with chemo,
and the priest
with his last rites
asks her religion.
None, she says,
then, smart-ass to the last,
spells it for him:
n-u-n.

Because of this,
my grandmother
spent her last days bitching
up a storm: the sage had turned
the cornbread dressing
gourd green, nothing tasted right.
She wept
big, unreasonable toddler
tears. *We worked so hard
on it,* she said, *and still, we got the dressing
all wrong. I know I'll never taste
Thanksgiving again
in all my life.*

At the time, I wanted
to be that family
reciting poems
to beckon
angels to drop blazing
beams of light
by her bed. I wanted
to pipe-in the pluck
of harmonious song,
wanted us to
genuflect, to cross
an *X* or two into the air

to scissor a passage
for her into the sky.
But no.
Hell, no.
Instead, we let her cry

            for a minute then said she
            couldn't kick the bucket, no,
          not now, because Bernie May
            wouldn't have a job
           no more, because everybody
          knows that woman would
        rather pick her toes than work,
         because that woman's too
      lazy to make a dime on her own.
       Bernie said, *You got that right,*
          told her, *Scoot your big*
           ass over in that bed.

You motherfuckers,
my grandmother said,
wiping her eyes. She took
the dry green dressing
to her dry mouth,
unable to swallow right
from laughing.

Fanny Says Again the Same Dream on Morphine

And they had long, black tails that went like this, on a sailboat, two animals, and I said, *You're beautiful.* And they were white, with long tails, and with white fox faces. Just beautiful. Do you know what kind of animal it coulda been? I just couldn't figure it out. It weren't no dog, no. And it weren't no cat neither. No. Nothing as big as no damn horse. I don't know what they were. I just knowed they was beautiful. And when I returned to the boat one of them was dead and I was scared and I sat on the dark edge but I didn't cry. No. I didn't cry at all. I crouched down there in that dark yard and just waited for somebody to come for me.

Flitter

is what she said but what she meant had nothing
to do with the lighting from one bloom to the next
by a monarch or an equally colorful diva at the bar.
What she meant was *your privates, your girlie parts,*
something you better soap up daily and watch
like a spectacled hawk. It was code, really,

a kid-friendly word like every Christ-fearing family has,
something to sidestep the gynecological *genitals*
and its speculum-chilled *vagina*, something that wasn't
her *sex*—a word that said *Colette*, both verb and noun
exhaling the same thin gentlewoman cigar.
Hers was a word rated PG, something that wasn't once

an innocent kitty in boots that now swung
practically buck-naked from a pole, and never do you hear
flitter in any bass-thumping salt-and-pepper-my-mango,
va-jay-jay songs. No. *Flitter* is lyrical but awkward; despite
its featherweight meaning, it never does fly.
To me, *flitter* sounds heavy, ironic, with the phonic
aptitude of a frying pan, a word a little *too* natural perhaps,
in need of a shave.

What kept it alive was that "f" sound, slightly transgressive,
ready to leap off the four-letter cliff, but more so it echoed
with *fat* and *flat,* the two qualities of a flitter Fanny found.
A babygirl, for example, was always born with *a fat flitter,*
and that's exactly what she would be called,
then there was *fat as a flitter,* applying to cute, chunky things
like chipmunk cheeks and toddler's wrists and puppy dogs.

Then, of course, there was *flat,* a more mature version
of the same, and if you did enough crunches, yes,
your belly would be *flat as a flitter.* The similes go on,
as carbonated beverages can go *flat as a flitter,* as can your hair
on a humid day, and if you drive west, all that land—you got it—
flitter-flat.

My favorite times with the word were the last days
we had her, when she needed oxygen and ice chips
and kept death backed into a corner
by calling me *a flitterhead.* I swore I didn't have her remote,
and she didn't believe me until she found it
under the covers between her legs. She changed the channel,
said, *Okay, flitterhead. I'm sorry; right there was the clicker,
right under my flitter, who would have thought.* And when it was time
to change her, to wipe off the blackest

stool with a warm cloth, she kept me from deep
sorrow by saying, *Make sure to hit my bald flitter now—nobody tells you
every hair falls out down there as you age—and hit it with a douse
of powder, Koey, Grandma's gotta stay fresh.* I cleaned her as I would
a baby, turning her best I could from side to side, and later,
when I tired, I called in the nurse to help me hold her

so I could change the sheets. The nurse was from an island
not far from Florida but far enough that when our work was done,
she stopped me, asked, *I'm sorry. Your grandmother—I can't understand her.
Can you tell me what language she speaks?*

That was when I knew.
I wasn't losing my grandmother, no, I was losing
my home, the one place I could understand
the world through a mother tongue only she
could sing.

Fanny Asks Me a Question Before I'd Even Ask Myself

Now, my sister and her husband still do—every morning at five o'clock in the a.m. And the night she got married she said they did it fourteen times. And I believe her too. And I said, *Honey, it's a wonder you got a puss hair one, no wonder you ain't rubbed it all off,* and you know, I don't even think I could walk, but no, she said her and him did all night and woke up the next afternoon at 4:00. She got up to pee and he got up to pee and then they did it all over again. But he ain't never strayed from her, not one time. And it's a good thing too, because it would have broken her heart. . . . And it's a good thing he married her when he did—she had just turned fifteen (they had to walk across the bridge to Indiana to do so)—because like my daddy said to my mama oncet: *Monk, we gonna haveta watch that girl, we're gonna have to whup her; she's gonna be a slut.*

We called it *hot pants.* I don't know how she got so sexual. I just wished I had a bit of it. I think my mama had it too: my daddy let it kinda slip before she shut him up. But I never really did. Now, I do know my sister used to watch me and Monroe through the attic window. . . . It was a real ornery thing to do in them days, and I was embarrassed to death. Said she couldn't see nothing like our naked bodies or nothing but only them covers, *just a movin,* she said.

But I never was sexual like her. And I don't know why you aren't.

You ain't a lesbian, are you?

Well, okay. I'm just checking.

My Book, in Birds

A book of birds. A story in birds. Each breath
a bird, each dream slipped from my ear

to my pillow out the window a song:
cardinals laughing at me—*birdie birdie birdie*—

on a lonely Valentine's. Then robins swarming
the last bits of red another February day,

so many of them on the holly tree the branches
tick with their picking and I stop

the car. But I was so cold, I had to get to the store,
and in the fluorescent buzz of the freezer aisle, I swore

I heard, *A flock of larks is called an exaltation*,
but thought, *No, that's too pretty, that can't be*

right. I bought my frozen pizza and peas and tried to
remember warmer days:

the surf shop with the parrot, big and green with a beak
full of fingers, my hair a dread of salt and seaweed

so I would run home
to wash the sand from my scalp. In the shower,

on the sill of the window made to crank tightly closed
to hurricanes, her porcelain bluebird—

all those years, Fanny swore she'd die and come back
red-breasted, blue-winged, and singing,

but when the time came, it was only morphine
talking: white beasts stalking the hospital room,

*with tails long as a Cadillac and tail feathers flowing like new
curtains*, she said, *and faces, they've got faces bright and sharp as a fox.*

There was nothing I could do. The reincarnation
I used to believe in became a drag queen named Phoenix

on Saturday nights at the bar where a girl leaned in
to me with both thumbs cowboy-hooked

to the pockets of her jeans, nothing more.
When she asked for my number, I made for the door.

There was nothing I could do and so I traveled
to Brooklyn where birds sing louder, competing

against sirens and cabs and ice cream trucks.
I tried to find a woman there who made me forget

the woman before, the one who took me
to a red barn, swallows knifing

the air between rafters. I left her,
I always left, my heart a young hummingbird

that learned hummingbirds land
but never really stay—only fledglings

hesitate at the red plastic feeder. I said, *I just can't,*
I said it, then left, said it,

then made my way to that stone marking
the death of my grandmother. Her ashes are not

there, but her name is, and because I still believed
in some words, it was enough. I went there to seek

permission, to cool my face against the granite and ask,
Is what I have become okay?

After, I fed the cemetery swans dandelion greens
and thought their beauty not unlike the hissing

swan of Lake Bled, the tidal swan of Galway, all
water the same drowning, no matter how far I go.

Once I had the courage, I took another woman
to my bed but woke on the porch

to a cathedral of sunrise singing, the boards splintered
hard to my back. I walked with her

to the park where a yellow bird followed alongside
in a sine cosine rollercoaster of flight.

I argued with her—*It's not possible, a canary
in Kentucky*—but thought, *Why not?*

What's lovely in this world is no more impossible
than what's not—when I was married

to a man, three sparrows trapped themselves in that porch light
and cooked against the glass; later that first summer

as a wife, a mother jay—again, say it—*trapped*
in the garden pond, my face reflected in that fish-shit water

dashed bright
with blue feathers and golden koi.

I never did grow old enough with him
for the pink plastic flamingos to decorate the front yard,

never did see that hokey sign—*Lordie, Lordie,*
look who's forty!—and it made me cry like a peacock and shred

my flesh in strips to the black tower
beaks—*Take it, dear raven. Take it,*

clacking black crow. When there was no meat
left, I threw strands of hair and bits of cheap bread

to fast-food sparrows, ate for years on the bland sorrow
of grease and plastic and frustrated men

until I traveled to a woman who had a lilac-eyed
cockatoo that beat its head against my collarbone

to rush up a serving of hot fruit and seed, a vomit offering
meant for another with a beak to guzzle it

back down. I said, *I'm sorry, but I think your bird*
is sick, but she simply cleaned

off my shirt, put her pet softly back
in the cage. *No, baby, that's her way of saying*

she loves you, she said. *Can't you tell*
love from sickness?

A Translation for the Spiritual Mediator
Who May Speak for Me to Frances Lee Cox,
Wherever She May Be

Original:
Fanny, somebody's laying on their horn this morning
right outside your window. I just sat down to get
through to you, but he's out there, hollering his ass off.
So how I'm supposed to do this?

Translation:
Grandmother, I should not speak to the dead,
but I'm lonely. Yesterday afternoon I slept, hot-dreaming
of a baby that wouldn't stop crying in my arms. It was mine,
that baby, and its hunger was all I needed in this world.

Original:
Fanny, you would throw a fit. That stupid fucking EMS done tore up your
carpet with their heavy boots, and Butchie had to tape up your mirrored
closet door where they cracked it trying to get you outta here. I don't know
what their big rush was anyways, considering. I been windexing and
cloroxing since I got here Thursday, but ain't a thing I can do for that carpet
except rip it up.

Translation:
Grandmother, your son Butch pulled your dentures out for
drops of nitroglycerin and—because he didn't know better—
a desperate last phenobarbital. It was two on a Sunday
afternoon and the tumor in your abdomen had pushed your
heart up so far it
         couldn't anymore.

That ambulance raced you to the hospital to run tests to prove
what we already knew. It was paperwork, really, pushing it

through in order for the state to wrap things up.
Hospice picked up your bed the very next morning
and sent a nurse to count and collect all unused pills.

Original:

Butchie is just about the sweetest fucker I ever did see. Did you know
he ran up to Publix yesterday just to get me everything to make macaroni
and cheese—slow-cooked, casserole-style? Now you know and I know that
milk was just a makin him gag, but he did it anyways.
He's trying, Fanny. He's trying.

Translation:

Your lactose-intolerant son. Your son who cleared out
every single item in your refrigerator after you were gone
but refused to let anyone move
anything else.
Your one-armed reading glasses, your
extra-large bottle
of extra-strength Tylenol, your rhinestone writing pen.
Your hair rollers and your Quick Tan and your Merit
Ultra Lights. Your gun.
All still on your nightstand.
He's drinking again, and heavy, and last night he was already asleep
when it was still light outside and still asleep when I got home.
He's trying. Jesus, is he trying.

Original:

Don't you fuss at me. I ain't seeing that boy
no more, and I did just what you said to do:
I kept my head high and walked right past.

Translation:

The one I was with made me sour and turn
cold. I held on for a month or two,
hoping, but I never want them long. With men,
I am a rattling gourd, a dry song.

Original:

I got Uncle Tony's class ring for him, and for Mama
I'll bring your rolling pin and flour sifter. For myself
I'm collecting little things that might help me remember,
like your Aqua Filters and one of them 16-ounce plastic glasses
you like for your Pepsi. I'm taking an article too
I found in your underwear drawer,
the one about Pleasant Grove and that river you were baptized in.
And oh, yeah, I'm taking this lavender scarf.
I hope you don't mind, I thought I just might wear it
in my hair when the weather turns this spring.

Translation:

It is not enough. I cannot describe you,
lay you flat
on this page
with words.
The palm fronds beyond your window have grown
thick enough that no one could possibly see in
from the outside now.

To My Grandmother's Ghost, Flying with Me on a Plane

For if there's nothing then
        nothing. And if there's something
                then there's something. Say it
                        again: if there's nothing, then
nothing, and if something,
        something. This is ablution:
                a curl of a cousin's hand
                        into a blackened fiddlehead,
the mirror shattered on your
        closet door. This is the detritus
                left behind: something, something,
                        nothing, nothing, nothing, nothing.

I try to steady myself, say the Lord's
        Prayer as the wings crest above
                the city's capillaries of false light
                        so crowded this morning when I followed
a beautiful woman to the square.
        She stepped into the subway stairs
                and before disappearing turned,
                        said, *Come step into this dark*

hole in the ground with me?
        Fanny, she did not mean to be
                morbid. She only meant to say,
                      Follow me. And what I mean
is that I love her and did not
        follow. Fanny, the stewardess
                has nothing on her rattling cart
                      to quench this thirst and the Sky

Mall does not comfort me tonight.
     Worse, I can see death either way:
          the velvet black of anesthesia, count back
             and you're nine, eight, seven, six, five,
gone, or something better, peacock-feathered,
     smelling of leather-bound books and you baking
          cornbread. I mean, will you come for me? Will you
             come get me, your hair piled high and white, when
it's my time to go? Or will I find
     you another kind of mother,
          the one who knows the dyke
             I've become? Will you be cross,
your face a streak of all my
     desire, telling me I was a fool
          to yearn to follow her? Or ashamed,
             will you turn away your face and hold up
a shard
     of that mirror,
          showing me
             I'm going to hell?

Fanny Linguistics: Thaumatology

There are words I want to give
        you now, Fanny, words that
might have eased your way.

Words for trees,
        not just *tree*
but *Sycamore* & *Beech* & *Cypress*,

words that make that "b" in *subtlety*
        make sense, words that make
differences into *dimensions*,

that make *salt*—
        just about your only savory spice—
into *coriander* & *cilantro* & *saffron*.

I want to give you *geophagy*—
        a word for those women you knew—
the ones who ate dirt—then tell you

about the work I've done—
        years of geophagy—
marrying catsup & collating & kneading crust,

and once even when I was paid
        to think—paid to run the meeting—I was scolded
for not making the coffee right.

I want to whisper *thaumatology*—
        the study of miracles—
because outside this cabin is a forest:

deer moss & *sand berries* & *White Pine*
      trees that drop the weight they don't need
as they age. Imagine

even hummingbirds here, Fanny,
      gray ones no bigger than a thumb
suckling tiger lilies, right outside the door.

A miracle, because inside
      I am warm, my own pot of coffee on;
I've got nothing to do today

but write you &
      write down
what you say.

The Family Celebrates Independence

It's the 4th, the sky at noon already hungover with gunpowder and the birds frightened from their roost. It's the 4th, the family without Fanny but still talk talk talking of Fanny. The family piles out with plastic forks and paper plates and paper towels, the family piles out with deviled eggs and macaroni salad and Benedictine and chips. It's the 4th, and Mama's husband's grilling a 24-pack of franks, ten pounds of hamburger, and *one veggie burger for miss tree-hugger here.* It's the 4th, the heat so intense even the uncle with the glass eye church-fans himself under the ginkgo tree, *Hot damn, it's the 4th.*

It's the 4th, and the little purse dog dressed especially for the occasion in a striped doggie dress is shitting and shaking; the aunt with all the gold bracelets tries to calm him as you would an autistic child—with compression, tight wrapped in a kitchen towel. She's begging the boys to lay off the bottle rockets, *You boys are about to kill Pookie here.* It's the 4th, and *We need another bag of ice;* it's the 4th, and *Somebody get more beer. Damn it if I told you once already will somebody move the ice-cream maker? That salt's going to ruin my lawn.* It's the 4th, and *Has anybody seen the baby? I hear the baby crying.* It's the 4th, and the baby is screaming Darth-Vader-style into a box fan—*Will somebody watch the baby's fingers?* and *Is that my glass? Has anyone seen my glass? Where's my pocketbook? Do you think that mayonnaise might be carny by now? Well, pitch that shit before we all get sick; we only got one toilet here.*

It's the 4th, and the tall cousin is getting taller and the fat cousin is getting fatter, *Bless her heart;* it's the 4th, and the pretty aunt with big teeth nurses a cup of milk for her throat. It's the 4th, and the cousin with the dragon tattooed on his thigh shoots tree frogs with a pellet gun; his wife is pregnant again, grinning hard as a suck-egg dog. And somebody says, *Where does that come from anyway—suck-egg dog?* and *Hell if I know,* the cousin says, *but she sure is craving deviled eggs; she's had five already.*

It's the 4th, and *Doesn't anyone have an Alka-Seltzer? Tylenol? Rolaid? Band-Aid? Serving spoon? Tommy Tippee Cup for the baby? Where is the baby? Has anyone seen the baby? Good god, precious angel, step away from that fan, you're about to cut off every one of your fingers.* It's the 4th, and for one day this summer, even the conductor must have a day off: The train's not howling down the tracks, and the neighbor's wolf hybrid isn't chained and snarling through the fence, and Mama's got on her bra, for company's sake. It's the 4th, and *Some genius brought red, white, and blue cupcakes. Who thought blue icing was a good idea on these white counters? Specially with all these messy kids, they eat one after another, look at that baby with its blue mouth, watch his fingers on that box fan.*

It's firecrackers and bottle rockets before dusk, and after, it's Roman candles brought over the state line; it's the kind uncle with the whiskey sweats spitting chew into one beer can and drinking from another. It's the 4th, and *Does anybody want to take home this fruit salad? Cause we'll never eat all this fruit. Now, lettuce you can feed to the your chickens, take that, but those onions, mercy, those onions are too fucking strong. Nobody wants them onions. Throw those out, but here, take a pie home—cherry or apple, take your pick—and this taco salad's been out too long. Throw it out too. If somebody gives me a black plastic bag, I can pick up these cans, and look, the neighbors have already started in: Hear that little dog just a howling. That was a good one—all them purdy colors—there goes another one in green. Where is the baby? Okay, somebody take him in. Don't you dare give him a sparkler, he'll burn himself to ashes and a puddle of grease. Take him on in, that diaper's ripe. Ain't that ice cream ready yet? Anybody seen my keys?* and *Damn it to hell, shew have mercy if I don't have some heartburn now.*

Boy, them fireworks sure are beautiful, don't you think?

An Invitation for My Grandmother

Satisfaction is a lowly / thing, how pure a thing is joy. / This is mortality / this is eternity.
—Marianne Moore

When Mama called to say you were
gone, I was in New York and climbed
the impossible top of a brownstone to talk
myself down. *Don't get sentimental; dying is what*
grandmother's do, was what
I told myself, but what I should have done
was invite you there with me. You'd never been
further north than Cincinnati, and the view—
the spatter and fleck of all those lights—
you'd have to see to believe. So now that you're

on the other side and got your knees working
again, a proposition: Come, lace up your Keds,
walk with me awhile. I won't say the world's better—
it's not—since you left, I've seen a pelican
stretch her wings to dry, the dripping
petrol making her into a bent crucifix of oil,
and the penguins have dropped their proud
eggs into melted ice, and this spring, yet another wind
bulldozed my neighbors, all their homes razed
to slab foundation, their trees now
splintered bone. But we can take a train

out of here—Come, sit next to me,
because out the window
a girl on a horse jumps a junkyard fence.
She wears a shirt the color of poppies, of bright
soda cans, and I bet you'll agree: blurred,
it is a brown pony with red wings.

And three years ago: Can I take you there?
My sister, sitting up during a contraction,
how she reached inside
herself to touch the crown of her son
not yet born. I want to show you the look
on her face and that cord
cut, a rich earth of blood, a thick black
joy. And please, take off your shoes now,

stand with me last October when
I took a wife, barefoot in the grass.
We made our vows, and after, when she held
my jaw with both hands, I could feel
the bones of my skull
rising up to make a face finally
seen.

A Prayer for the Self-Made Man

—for Monroe J. Cox

who lost his mother to tuberculosis and his father to drink,
who curled in doorways and boxcars until he found work hauling crates

to the market and sweeping the market floor, who grew enough to cradle
a black plum in his fist and eat it, two bites down,

who grew forearms big as a kid's thighs and took aim at a nail, sinking it,
a single blow. A prayer for the man, self-made, snatching up a bride of sixteen,

a girl so country he had to teach her—how not to smear red lipstick
when he comes home, how to keep the groceries cool by hanging them in a bag

out the window. For the locket he bought her—ten dollars, two weeks' pay—
because exhausted he fell asleep on the phone, and though it took two tries,

she flushed that necklace down. A prayer for the man who not only
learned to hammer but became a hammer, hammering the sun up,

hammering the light back down with its hot grit of shingles, so many blows
to hold together the raw frame of homes. A prayer for the man

who worked until his heart stopped then ripped out the oxygen tubes,
knocked down the nurse, and worked some more. A prayer for the man

who had his ribcage cracked open four times before he slowed but did not
stop, for that long purple scar, for the blood that would not fill him to pleasure

anymore. A prayer for his thumb and pointer, chewed off by a jigsaw,
for the numbers he never learned in school but swore he could use

to unlock the code of the Florida Lottery. For those yellow legal pads,
all twenty-six of them, filled with winning combinations, for that rectangular pencil,

sharpened with his fish knife. For the bass he pulled from the lake.
I was a girl, squatting behind the kumquat tree, I saw how first he slit

them open, yanking out the bubbling guts, then, the fish still jerking,
he lopped off their heads. I was young, I didn't know there was a kinder way—

a prayer then for the slop of pink dumped in the canal, for what I saw on his face
as he prepared the flesh she was expected to fry up and we were expected to eat.

A prayer for his anger, I think I might understand, a prayer for his ridged
teeth and knotty scalp, for his paint-speckled belt and paint-speckled watch.

Can you tell me what time it is, Grandfather? I have kept your gears wound;
I wear its huge face on my wrist. Put your ear to me: I want your ghost to hear

this ticking. I want your bones to know it is time now: lay it down.

For My Grandmother's Perfume, Norell

Because your generation didn't wear perfume
        but chose a scent—a signature—every day
                you spritzed a powerhouse floral with top
                        notes of lavender and mandarin, a loud
smell one part Doris Day, that girl-next-door
        who used Technicolor to find a way to laugh about
                husbands screwing their secretaries over lunch,
                        the rest all Faye Dunaway, all high drama
extensions of nails and lashes, your hair
        a breezy fall of bangs, a stiletto entrance
                that knew to walk sideways, hip first:
                        now, watch a *real* lady descend the stairs.

Launched in 1968, Norell
        was the 1950s tingling with the beginning
                of Disco; Norell was a housewife tired of gospel,
                        mopping her house to Stevie Wonder instead.

You wore so much of it, tiny pockets
        of your ghost lingered hours after you
                were gone, and last month, I stalked
                        a woman wearing your scent through
the grocery so long I abandoned
        my cart and went home. Fanny, tell me:
                How can manufactured particles carry you
                        through the air? I always express what I see,
but it was no photo that
        stopped and queased me to my knees.

After all these years, you were an invisible
        trace, and in front of a tower of soup cans

I was a simple animal craving the deep memory
                worn by a stranger oblivious of me. If I had courage,
the kind of fool I'd like to be,
        I would have pressed my face to her small
                shoulder, and with the sheer work of
                        two pink lungs, I would have breathed
enough to
        conjure
                you back
                        to me.

Fanny Says Goodbye

Now, Koey, we won't have no goodbyes now. You know better, and you make sure to lock that back door. Now, go on. You remember what I told you, and lock that back door.

Acknowledgments

I would like to thank the editors of the following publications in which these poems first appeared, often in different versions:

Broadsided Press: "Pepsi" (excerpt);
Cave Wall: "For My Grandmother's Feet, Swollen Again," "The Dead";
Central Arkansas Broadside Project: "Dixie Highway" (excerpt);
The Cortland Review: "A Translation for the Spiritual Mediator Who May Speak for Me to Frances Lee Cox, Wherever She May Be";
Ellipses: "To My Grandmother's Ghost, Flying with Me on a Plane," "Pheno";
Iron Horse Literary Review: "EPO," "Fanny Says at Twenty-three She Learned to Drive," "For My Grandmother's Teeth, Pulled When She Was Thirty-six";
JMWW: "Go Put on Your Face," "Your Monthly";
The Literary Review: "Crisco";
Los Angeles Review: "My Book, in Birds";
The Oxford American: "Fuck";
San Pedro Review: "A Prayer for the Self-Made Man";
storySouth: "Fanny Says How to Be a Lady," "Sweet Silver";
Tahoma Literary Review: "A Genealogy of the Word";
Waccamaw: "Hettie," "Pepsi";
The Wide Shore: "Clorox."

"For My Grandmother's Perfume, Norell" and "Fanny Linguistics: Nickole" were selected by the Academy of American Poets for their Poem-A-Day Project, and a nascent version of "Sweet Silver" appeared in *Wingbeats*, a craft anthology published by Dos Gatos Press in 2012. A version of "My Book, in Birds" won A Room of One's Own Foundation's Orlando Prize for Poetry in 2010, and Cornelius Eady chose "Clorox" as the winner of the Cultural Center of Cape Cod Poetry Competition in 2013.

Quotations are from the following sources:
    Allison, Dorothy. *Two or Three Things I Know for Sure*. New York: Penguin, 1995.
    Baldwin, James. "Stranger in the Village," *Notes of a Native Son*, New York: Beacon Press, 1955.

Moore, Marianne. "What Are Years?", *What Are Years*. New York: Macmillan, 1941.

O'Connor, Flannery. *Mystery and Manners: Occasional Prose*. New York: Farrar, Straus and Giroux, 1969.

I am indebted to my family for their support of this book, in particular my mother who gave me courage (who always gives me courage)—these stories here are not entirely mine to tell, but she lent me strength to put them to the page. I also want to thank her sister, my Aunt Toni, who, after reading the manuscript, called to say I did right by her mother's story. She's not one to hesitate to say exactly what she thinks, so although I know there is much I missed and perhaps got wrong, I take her at word. I would not have published these poems without their blessing. I would also like to dedicate this book, in part, to Ethel Pearl Graham, who helped raise me, and to the memory of my cousin, Eric Cox, who died tragically and too young.

I thank the late Kurt Brown and his wife Laure-Anne Bosselaar, my sweetest friend and best damn teacher I've ever had; and thanks to my longtime pal Raymond McDaniel who dished out some solid editorial (and life) advice when I needed it; and my dear friend, Nicole Pollitt, whose own mama could rival Fanny in just about anything. I also thank my little sisters Hope and Rachel, who help me remember, always (and took care to remind me that Fanny let them both try cigarettes before the age of ten). In addition, I extend gratitude to the many friends who've helped me these past ten years as this book took shape: Lisa Hunt, who leans into the world with a strength and kindness given to her by her own coffee-swigging granny; Leslie Wilson, who knows what it is to love a fierce grandmother fiercely; Travis Carmack, who still laughs with me over these old stories; Pee Wee Watson, who bought me airline tickets to visit Fanny those last few weeks of her life when I didn't have a dime to my name; Patricia Smith, who helped me navigate my most difficult poem in this book; Rebecca Gayle Howell, who always brings me back to my Kentucky home.

I also thank those that generously gave me a place to hide away and write: Katie Mead and Robert Alexander, for time and space in your cabin in almost-Canada, Michigan ("Fanny Linguistics: Thaumatology" is for you); Doug Melkovitz and Lee Fleming, for offering me your sweet cabin in way-out-where-no-one-will-find-me Arkansas; Dennis Maloney and Elaine LaMattina, for surrounding me with the beauty of Big Sur, a place so sacred I didn't dare waste a day. I'd also like to thank the English Department at the University of Arkansas at Little Rock, in particular Dean Deborah Baldwin and Trey Philpotts for the summer research grants that gave me time to revise these poems, and especially David Jauss, my colleague and longtime mentor. I also want to give a nod to my phenomenal gaggle of students—at UALR, Murray State, and Sewanee—for tolerating the fact that Fanny seems to boss her way into nearly every workshop I teach. I'd also like to mention Eloise Klein Healy: though you lost your words a few years ago, I know you'll recover. In the meantime, I still hear you talking to me, giving me the best advice an Arktoi bear could want.

I'd like to thank three organizations: First, the National Endowment for the Arts, because with their support, I was able to make the changes in my life that led to the completion of this book. Secondly, the Kentucky Foundation for Women—years ago, they lent me the encouragement to write down my grandmother's stories while I still had her, and it's no understatement to say that without their generosity, these poems would not exist. Finally, BOA Editions: Peter Conners, you convinced me to send you this manuscript, and it wasn't but a few months later that you wrote me about your own grandmother Bema, then sent me a contract. I can't quite believe my luck knowing you in this world. Sandy Knight, your design crafted a sweet cover in Fanny's color. Jenna Fisher and Melissa Hall, you two make a firecracker of a team up there in Rochester with Peter, and I can't thank you enough for your hard work. It's not easy birthing collections of poetry into the stream of books published each year, I know. You can always count on me for chocolates around Christmastime.

Finally, Jessica Jacobs—my reader, my witness, my wife. You've read these poems more times than anyone and, still, you believe in them. Your faith and love are a miracle.

About the Author

Nickole Brown grew up in Louisville, Kentucky, and Deerfield Beach, Florida. Her books include her debut, *Sister,* a novel-in-poems published by Red Hen Press in 2007, and an anthology, *Air Fare,* that she co-edited with Judith Taylor. She graduated from The Vermont College of Fine Arts, studied literature at Oxford University as an English Speaking Union Scholar, and was the editorial assistant for the late Hunter S. Thompson. She has received grants from the National Endowment for the Arts, the Kentucky Foundation for Women, and the Kentucky Arts Council. She worked at the independent, literary press, Sarabande Books, for ten years, and she was the National Publicity Consultant for Arktoi Books and the Palm Beach Poetry Festival. She has taught creative writing at the University of Louisville, Bellarmine University, and at the low-residency MFA Program in Creative Writing at Murray State and the Sewanee Young Writers' Conference. Currently, she is the Editor for the Marie Alexander Series in Prose Poetry at White Pine Press and is an Assistant Professor at University of Arkansas at Little Rock. She lives with her wife, poet Jessica Jacobs.

BOA Editions, Ltd. American Poets Continuum Series

No. 46 *Trillium*
Richard Foerster

No. 47 *Fuel*
Naomi Shihab Nye

No. 48 *Gratitude*
Sam Hamill

No. 49 *Diana, Charles, & the Queen*
William Heyen

No. 50 *Plus Shipping*
Bob Hicok

No. 51 *Cabato Sentora*
Ray Gonzalez

No. 52 *We Didn't Come Here for This*
William B. Patrick

No. 53 *The Vandals*
Alan Michael Parker

No. 54 *To Get Here*
Wendy Mnookin

No. 55 *Living Is What I Wanted: Last Poems*
David Ignatow

No. 56 *Dusty Angel*
Michael Blumenthal

No. 57 *The Tiger Iris*
Joan Swift

No. 58 *White City*
Mark Irwin

No. 59 *Laugh at the End of the World:
Collected Comic Poems 1969–1999*
Bill Knott

No. 60 *Blessing the Boats: New and Selected Poems:
1988–2000*
Lucille Clifton

No. 61 *Tell Me*
Kim Addonizio

No. 62 *Smoke*
Dorianne Laux

No. 63 *Parthenopi: New and Selected Poems*
Michael Waters

No. 64 *Rancho Notorious*
Richard Garcia

No. 65 *Jam*
Joe-Anne McLaughlin

No. 66 *A. Poulin, Jr. Selected Poems*
Edited, with an Introduction
by Michael Waters

No. 67 *Small Gods of Grief*
Laure-Anne Bosselaar

No. 68 *Book of My Nights*
Li-Young Lee

No. 69 *Tulip Farms and Leper Colonies*
Charles Harper Webb

No. 70 *Double Going*
Richard Foerster

No. 71 *What He Took*
Wendy Mnookin

No. 72 *The Hawk Temple at Tierra Grande*
Ray Gonzalez

No. 73 *Mules of Love*
Ellen Bass

No. 74 *The Guests at the Gate*
Anthony Piccione

No. 75 *Dumb Luck*
Sam Hamill

No. 76 *Love Song with Motor Vehicles*
Alan Michael Parker

No. 77 *Life Watch*
Willis Barnstone

No. 78 *The Owner of the House: New Collected Poems
1940–2001*
Louis Simpson

No. 79 *Is*
Wayne Dodd

No. 80 *Late*
Cecilia Woloch

No. 81 *Precipitates*
Debra Kang Dean

No. 82 *The Orchard*
Brigit Pegeen Kelly

No. 83 *Bright Hunger*
Mark Irwin

No. 84 *Desire Lines: New and Selected Poems*
Lola Haskins

No. 85 *Curious Conduct*
Jeanne Marie Beaumont

No. 86 *Mercy*
Lucille Clifton

No. 87 *Model Homes*
Wayne Koestenbaum

No. 88 *Farewell to the Starlight in Whiskey*
Barton Sutter

No. 89 *Angels for the Burning*
David Mura

No. 90 *The Rooster's Wife*
Russell Edson

No. 91 *American Children*
Jim Simmerman

No. 92 *Postcards from the Interior*
Wyn Cooper

No. 93 *You & Yours*
Naomi Shihab Nye

No. 94 *Consideration of the Guitar:
New and Selected Poems 1986–2005*
Ray Gonzalez

Colophon

BOA Editions, Ltd., a not-for-profit publisher of poetry and other literary works, fosters readership and appreciation of contemporary literature. By identifying, cultivating, and publishing both new and established poets and selecting authors of unique literary talent, BOA brings high-quality literature to the public. Support for this effort comes from the sale of its publications, grant funding, and private donations.

The publication of this book is made possible, in part,
by the special support of the following individuals:

Anonymous x 2
Armbruster Family Foundation
Bernadette Catalana, *in memory of Richard Calabrese*
Michael Hall
Sandi Henschel, *in honor of my dear friend Boo Poulin*
John C. Jacob
Jack & Gail Langerak
Barbara & John Lovenheim
Edith Matthai, *in memory of Peter Hursh*
Boo Poulin, *in honor of Sandi Henschel*
Deborah Ronnen & Sherman Levey
Steven O. Russell & Phyllis Rifkin-Russell
David W. Ryon
Michael Waters & Mihaela Moscaliuc